9.⁶⁰

# Nurture *the* Heart, Feed *the* World

Leon Hesser

Nurture the Heart, Feed the World

ISBN: 0-9744668-8-3

Published by

Synergy Books

2525 W Anderson Lane, Suite 540
Austin, Texas 78757

Tel: 512.407.8876
Fax: 512.478.2117

info@bookpros.com
http://www.bookpros.com

*To the Memory of*
*Captain Fremont P. Koch, M.D.*
*Mentor extraordinaire*

# Contents

# About Norman Borlaug
## who wrote the Foreword for this Book

Dr. Norman E. Borlaug was awarded the Nobel Peace Prize in 1970 for his pioneering research that led to the Green Revolution in the 1960s. He is rightfully credited with having saved millions of people in developing countries from starvation – more than any other one person in history. He is revered in much of Asia, Africa and Latin America. For all that, Norman Borlaug is hardly a household name in America. He should be.

Borlaug was born on an Iowa farm in 1914. At the University of Minnesota, he earned a Bachelor of Science degree in 1937, a master's degree in 1939 and a doctorate in plant pathology in 1942. Following a stint with E. I. du Pont de Nemours Foundation, he was hired in 1944 by The Rockefeller Foundation to organize and direct the Wheat Research and Production program in Mexico, in cooperation with the Government of Mexico. As described in Chapter One of this book, by the mid-1960s his high-yielding varieties of wheat were being introduced in other countries, with dramatic results, most notably in the hungry nations of India and Pakistan.

Dr. Borlaug has been honored with more than 40 honorary doctorate degrees and numerous awards by governments, academic institutions and citizens' groups worldwide. He continues to work tirelessly – in his battle against starvation he makes several trips each year to Africa from his base in Mexico. On March 26, 2004 he called the author of this book from Mexico and said, "Leon, I didn't get much work done yesterday – it was hectic around here; they celebrated my 90th birthday!"

## Foreword

*Nurture the Heart, Feed the World* sheds light on one of the basic challenges facing world decision-makers: How should societies organize to feed the growing populations of the planet Earth?

Despite predictions of mass starvation by doomsayers, progress toward meeting the challenge in the 20th century was generally quite good. True, there were scattered pockets of hunger in the world, due mainly to uneven distribution patterns and natural disasters. But mass starvation was averted and most people were reasonably well-fed.

Why did the doomsayers miss their predictions?

For one thing, they didn't understand the power of the new technologies that would serve as a catalyst in situations in which other key ingredients were present. Pakistan in the late 1960s, for example, had an irrigated area in the Punjab of 28 to 30 million acres, leading farmers were beginning to use fertilizer and, importantly, an international group of advisors were working together as a team to help introduce the new technologies. This team consisted of representatives of the Ford Foundation, the Rockefeller Foundation, the Harvard Advisory Group, and a number of technical and administrative staff in the U.S. Agency for International Development (USAID).

Leon Hesser, as Chief of the Agriculture Division, was one of the key members of the USAID Mission. I first met Leon when I was in Karachi in early 1966. Shortly after that meeting, Leon and his staff pulled off an event that helped spark the Green Revolution in West Pakistan. That remarkable story is told in Chapter One of this book.

The Ford and Rockefeller foundations deserve much of the credit for the rapid increases in the world's food supplies. Their leadership had the vision. They pinned hopes on the development of new and improved agricultural production technologies and they supported highly focused research efforts of the kind that evolved into the Maize and Wheat Improvement Center

(CIMMYT) in Mexico and the International Rice Research Institute (IRRI) in the Philippines. These two centers served as models for a dozen more that were started in the 1970s.

International agricultural development assistance began in the early 1940s, thanks in no small measure to the efforts of my friend Henry A. Wallace, who had been Secretary of Agriculture and then Vice President to Franklin Roosevelt. In 1943, Wallace helped convince the Rockefeller Foundation to establish the first U.S. foreign agricultural assistance program – the Mexican Government-Rockefeller Foundation Cooperative Agricultural program. I joined that program in 1944 as a young scientist assigned to wheat research and development. Within a decade, positive results were showing in wheat production in Mexico.

In his periodic visits to Mexico, Wallace expressed interest in the new semi-dwarf wheats and their potential to revolutionize production in Asia. In 1963 he asked, "Are your new wheats going to make a difference in Asia?"

I responded, "Give us five years and South Asia will be self-sufficient in wheat production." As it turned out, this milestone was reached in 1968 in Pakistan and in 1972 in India. Sadly, Wallace did not live to see this happen.

During the last four decades of the 20th century, sweeping changes occurred in the factors of production used by farmers in many parts of the world, especially in much of Asia. Over this 40-year period, high-yielding semi-dwarf varieties increased to 84 and 74 percent, respectively, of the wheat and rice areas; irrigated areas more than doubled; fertilizer consumption increased more than 30-fold, and tractors replaced much of the animal power. The result: combined wheat and rice production increased from 127 million tons to 762 million tons annually.

Green Revolution critics have tended to focus too much on the wheat and rice varieties, per se, as if they alone can produce miraculous results. The fact is that modern, disease-resistant varieties can only achieve their genetic yield potential if systematic changes are also made in crop management: dates and rates of planting, fertilization, water management, and weed and pest control. Many of these crop management changes must be applied simultaneously if the genetic yield potential of modern varieties is to be fully realized. Introducing appropriate crop management regimes is the domain of national agricultural extension services and their advisors. This is one area in which Leon Hesser's team made a substantial contribution toward achieving the Green Revolution in Pakistan. The high-yielding seeds served as the catalyst, but the seeds were most effective when accompanied by appropriate crop management.

What about the future? The potential for further expansion in the arable land area is limited for most regions of the world – certainly for densely populated Asia and Europe. Only in sub-Saharan Africa and South America do large unexploited tracts exist, and only a fraction of this land should eventually come into agricultural production. In Asia, home of more than half of the world's people, very little uncultivated land is left. Indeed, some of the land, especially in South Asia, currently in production should be taken out of cultivation because of high susceptibility to soil erosion.

The International Food Policy Research Institute (IFPRI) estimates that more than 85 percent of future growth in cereal production must come from increasing yields on lands already in production. Such productivity improvements will require varieties with higher genetic yield potential and greater tolerance of drought, insects and diseases. To achieve these genetic gains, advances in both conventional and biotechnology research will be needed.

I have some concerns:

- During the past two decades, support to public research systems in the industrialized countries has seriously declined and support for international agricultural research has dropped so precipitously as to border on the disastrous.
- The United States spends 40 times more on the military than it does on overseas development assistance.
- Trends in foreign assistance for agricultural and rural development have been declining, not only in the U.S., but among many other donor countries and institutions as well.
- In 2000, the World Bank reported its lowest level of support to agriculture in its history.

These trends must be reversed.

In conclusion, 34 years ago in my acceptance speech for the Nobel Peace Prize, I said that the Green Revolution had won a temporary success in man's war against hunger, which if fully implemented could provide sufficient food for humankind through the end of the 20th century. This has happened. But I also warned that unless the frightening power of human reproduction was curbed, the success of the Green Revolution would be only ephemeral.

I now say that the world has the technology – either available or well advanced in the research pipeline – to feed a population of 10 billion people.

This compares with the world's population of 6 billion at the turn of the 21$^{st}$ Century and 1.6 billion when I was born in 1914. But a sustained combination of conventional breeding and biotechnology research will be needed to ensure that the genetic improvement of food crops continues at a pace sufficient to meet growing world populations.

Norman E. Borlaug

# Preface

My husband, Leon Hesser, is the author of this book. He wrote nearly every word; it's his voice. But, like so many endeavors during our almost six decades of married life, it has been a joint project. I provided oral and written ideas and was a loyal and sometimes severe critic.

This project was born in response to the many friends and acquaintances who have said, "You guys must write your life stories." As we wrote and reflected, we concluded that descriptions of our lifetime ventures might well serve as a stimulating challenge to others who desire more meaning in life. We truly have had fulfilling lives together or, as Leon might say in a less-than-saintly moment, "It's been a hell of a ride!"

Leon and I first met just three months before he left for the Army as an 18-year-old during World War II. In that mission, he was one of the few to have earned both the Combat Infantry Badge and the Combat Medics Badge before he was 20. He doesn't talk about it; it's a matter of record.

Leon observed cultures in the Philippines and Japan that differed drastically from those of his Midwest farm heritage; this changed his perspective on life. We were married shortly after he returned from the war. We began as Indiana tenant farmers; we had two children. When he was 30, with encouragement from me, Leon sold his farm business and entered Purdue University as a freshman. By age 37 he had earned a Ph.D. in Agricultural Economics.

With encouragement from Leon, I started as a freshman at age 35. I received a BA in the same ceremony in which Leon got his Ph.D. Purdue also awarded me a PHT: Putting Hubby Through. I ultimately earned a doctorate in education.

We went to Pakistan in 1966 where Leon was Foreign Service Officer in the Agency for International Development, U.S. Department of State, in charge of agricultural technical assistance. In association with Norman Borlaug, 1970 Nobel Peace Prize laureate, he helped spark the Green Revolution that relieved hunger for the masses in South Asia. He then was assigned to Washington as director of the U.S. government's worldwide technical assistance to increase food production in poorer countries.

For 20 years, I was professor at The George Washington University and director of the Reading Center. In this preface, I mention but two of the many exciting events during those two decades. I met often with President and Mrs. Carter while Amy Carter was in the Center's after-school program for four years. At the request of the Saudi Royal Family, we replicated the Reading Center in Saudi Arabia where I was hosted by members of the Royal Family, including a visit in the palace with Queen Iffat who, during the mid-20th century, had been the champion of education for girls.

After retiring from State Department, as a consultant until he turned 75, Leon led teams to outline strategies to increase food production in some 20 countries of Asia, Africa, and Eastern Europe and helped transform state-owned collective farms in Ukraine to private ownership by the farms' workers.

We remain active in civil affairs in our retirement community in sunny Naples, Florida, where we enjoy the early morning sights and sounds of this delightful paradise.

Florence E. Hesser
January 2004

# Chapter One

# Culture Shock and the Green Revolution

The midnight lights of Karachi shone brightly as Pan Am flight # 2 circled to land, suggesting that the city was as alive as any western metropolis in the middle of the night. Yet, there was a difference: the city, strung out for miles along the coast of the Indian Ocean, was devoid of skyscrapers. And rather than six to ten lanes of congested vehicular traffic, only a few cars were interspersed among many camels bearing heavy loads. In a euphoric reaction to this adventure out of a page in *The Arabian Nights*, 12-year-old George Hesser observed from the air that the caravans of camels as they plied the city's streets looked like columns of ants.

What a contrast this was in the lives of Leon and Florence Hesser and their two children! A mere decade earlier the Hessers were young tenant farmers in the Midwest of the United States. Now, Leon was assigned for two years as Agricultural Economist in the USAID Mission to Pakistan; in a few weeks, he would be named Chief of the Agriculture Division with responsibility for managing U.S. technical assistance to help the country's millions of farmers in both East and West Pakistan increase food production – to move the country from near-starvation to a more plentiful food supply.

Leon had just finished six weeks of orientation at the U.S. Department of State in Washington, DC, to acquaint him with his new assignment with the United States Agency for International Development (USAID). During those six weeks, Florence had wound up her teaching assignment, had supervised the packing-out from their split-level home in Overland Park, Kansas, a suburb of Kansas City, and had driven their new 1966 Mustang from Kansas City to Washington with son George and 17-year-old daughter Gwendolyn.

The orientation also was intended to acquaint Leon with the new culture he was about to experience; the culture orientation was less successful than the technical one.

On the long drive from the Karachi Airport to their downtown hotel, the camels dutifully kept to the far left of the highway. A few months earlier Pakistan had tried to change to driving on the right side instead of the left, but they had to change back because the camels refused to walk on the right side.

Karachi and its environs were interesting in many ways: *bundar*-boat rides in the Indian Ocean, sea turtles nesting at night, the ruins of ancient Thatta in the desert, and a vintage church in which the Hessers soon became close friends with the head pastor, Bishop Amstutz, and his wife. They found a gifted and clever artist, Kohari, who would work several hours each week with Gwen who displayed a talent for painting. Leon fitted in quickly with his defined duties and filled in frequently for Chief of the Agriculture Division Chuck Elkinton while he was away from the office. But it was an entirely different kind of atmosphere from that at the Kansas City Federal Reserve Bank, where Leon had worked for three years after earning a Ph.D. at Purdue. Comparatively speaking, it was frantic. And Karachi was different from anything the Hessers had experienced before. All four of them were in culture shock. Florence felt left out of anything stimulating.

Leon says, "If we could have gone back to Kansas City at the end of six weeks without having to pay our transportation both ways we would have."

After a year in Pakistan, Leon had to fill out a Completion of Assignment Report (COAR) indicating what his preferences were for assignment after the two-year tour. He and Florence talked it over and agreed quickly that they preferred Kansas City. Leon so indicated on the COAR; he would resign from the Foreign Service when the two years were up. The Director of the USAID Mission, Bill Kontos, and Leon's immediate supervisor, Deputy Director Ernie Stern, both tried to convince Leon to take home leave at the end of the two years and return for a second tour. By that time Leon had been promoted to replace Chuck Elkinton as head of the Agency's agricultural development programs in both East and West Pakistan. Leon said, "No, my mind is made up; we're going back to Kansas City."

Amir Ahmed Khan, Secretary of Agriculture for the Government of West Pakistan, was one of the finest men and among the most effective administrators Leon had ever worked with. When the Secretary learned of Leon's decision to return to Kansas City he wrote a long letter dated January 30, 1968 to George Clay, President of the Federal Reserve Bank of Kansas City, in which he said in part:

*Secretary of Agriculture and Mrs. Amir Ahmed Khan*
*welcome the Hesser family to Pakistan*

*Dear Mr. President:*

*Dr. Leon F. Hesser . . . has been assisting the Government of Pakistan for the past two years in its efforts to become self-sufficient in food grains. . . . Dr. Hesser has been the Director of the Agriculture Wing of the Technical Assistance Programme in the US AID Mission to Pakistan that has been very influential in the rapid yields increases per acre of our major agricultural crops in Pakistan. US AID's contribution with its technical know-how and economic assistance in key areas is recognized throughout our nation by our President on down to the farmer who tills the soil. Dr. Hesser has been the key person in these efforts.*

*It is only recently that I have discovered that Dr. Hesser is planning to return to the US and leave us just at the time when his efforts are beginning to bear fruit and also at a time when our success will require his expert guidance. . . .*

*I request you to permit Dr. Hesser to spend at least one more year with us. . . . If you can see fit to release him for another year I can assure you that a nation of farmers and especially a struggling Secretary of Agriculture will be extremely grateful.*

*With warmest regards,*
*Yours sincerely,*
*(A. A. Khan)*

The Secretary's letter was too late. Arrangements had already been made for Leon's replacement to be transferred from South Korea. Joe Motherall, senior USAID agriculture officer in South Korea, was to arrive in time to overlap with Leon for a month before he and the family were to leave for Kansas City. Motherall arrived as scheduled. On his second night in the country Curry Brookshier, Leon's deputy for West Pakistan, had a small party to introduce Motherall to A. A. Khan. While the Secretary did not imbibe, he was accustomed to being at parties where others did. It turned out that six-foot-two Joe Motherall was an alcoholic. After a couple of drinks beyond what he may have had at home before coming to the party, with a slurred tongue he made some disparaging remarks. In an engaging discussion with A.A. Khan, who was smaller than average in stature, Joe looked down at him and said "Small potatoes are hard to peel." Then, in reaction to the Secretary's polite response, he said, "Don't give me that shit!" Curry and Leon were dumbfounded.

The next morning, Curry reported the incident in writing to Bill Kontos who said, "This man has got to go!"

A few days later, Bill Kontos and Ernie Stern summoned Leon to the Director's office. Bill said, "Leon, I have arranged with Washington for Joe Motherall to be transferred to Afghanistan. Is there any way we can entice you to stay on here after home leave?"

By this time exciting things were happening in Pakistan.

Leon said, "Let me talk with Florence and think about it over the week-end."

Among the exciting events was the beginning of what came to be known as the Green Revolution. A few weeks after the Hessers arrived in Karachi, Norman Borlaug strolled into Leon's office.

Dr. Borlaug was the Rockefeller Foundation scientist in charge of research on higher yielding varieties of wheat at the International Center for Wheat and Maize Improvement (CIMMYT) in Mexico. Norm made frequent round-the-world trips to counsel with scientists in a number of developing countries that were collaborating in the research. He briefed Leon on the implications for Pakistan of CIMMYT's research on wheat.

One variety – Lerma Rojo – a short-straw, high-yielding variety that had been developed at CIMMYT and tested in collaboration with Pakistan's scientists, met most of the criteria desired by Pakistani consumers, with one major exception: it was a red wheat. Pakistanis preferred white wheat. A sizable quantity of the high-yielding Lerma Rojo had been imported earlier from Mexico; the seed had been multiplied and had the potential of moving Pakistan toward self-sufficient within the next two to three years. That was indeed exciting.

But the endearing Dr. Borlaug had more news, equally as exciting. He and his colleagues at CIMMYT had developed a wheat – a sort of sister variety to Lerma Rojo – that produced white grains. It was almost perfect for Pakistani tastes.

"But," Dr. Borlaug lamented, "only a small quantity of seed of this new variety is currently available."

Borlaug then emphasized that while the new seeds developed under his direction at CIMMYT had the inherent genetic capacity to increase yields dramatically, to achieve the potential required better husbandry, including higher applications of fertilizer, than Pakistani farmers were accustomed to. The new seed varieties could serve as a catalyst, but farmer education and a radically improved fertilizer distribution system were needed. He pleaded for USAID's collaboration.

After the meeting with Borlaug, Leon spent about two months gathering information and interviewing key agricultural officials. Then he wrote two documents that, as it turned out, were instrumental in helping achieve the Green Revolution. The first document was an analysis of Pakistan's fertilizer production and distribution system. In short, the paper made the case that it was time to transfer responsibility for fertilizer distribution from the government's agricultural extension service to the private sector. USAID's Mission Director presented the paper to Pakistan's Minister of Development who passed it to President Ayub Khan who said, "Let's do it!"

And they did.

*Dr. Norman E. Borlaug*
*"Father of the Green Revolution"*
*and Nobel Peace Prize laureate, 1970*

In the process of gathering information, Leon learned through an extended network that an enterprising private farmer in Mexico had somehow acquired some seed of the promising new variety, the white-kernel sister to Lerma Rojo, and had proceeded surreptitiously to multiply it. Curry Brookshier, who had shared this intelligence with A. A. Khan, asked Leon on behalf of the Secretary whether it might be possible to acquire some of that seed.

Leon spent a few more days analyzing the situation. It seemed that conditions were right in West Pakistan for a breakthrough in wheat production: the irrigation system covered nearly 30 million acres; fertilizer use had been introduced and its use was accepted by a few leading farmers; Punjabi farmers in the irrigated area were ready to take on a new technology if it promised more than a 20 percent increase in yields; Borlaug had successfully charged high-level government officials to the possibility of a much-needed breakthrough; and Curry Brookshier had a dozen agricultural extension advisors on his team who needed a shot in the arm – a catalyst. With potential yields that were double or even triple those of native varieties, Borlaug's new wheat varieties were the needed catalyst.

In doing his background work Leon learned that the Ford Foundation had recently contracted with Ignacho Narvaez, an agronomist who had been associated with Mexico's wheat development program, to serve as wheat production advisor to West Pakistan. Nacho was stationed at Lahore. He had already become close friends with Curry Brookshier and his agricultural extension advisors, including Staley Pitts, who were also stationed at Lahore. Together, they would constitute a formidable team of advisors.

Leon wrote a justification for a $25,000 grant to procure about 50 tons of the new white-kernel wheat from the Mexican farmer. The American ambassador, who had authority to approve grants of this size, signed off. Brookshier called Staley Pitts, who was now on home leave in Arizona, and said, "Staley, get your ass down in Mexico and buy 50 tons of that new white wheat and get it over here in time to plant this fall."

Staley was a no-nonsense, former-football-coach sort of guy. He flew down to Mexico and negotiated with the farmer: "I'll give you a good price for 50 tons of this wheat delivered on the other side of the border in Texas – you figure out how to get it over there." Staley knew better than to get tangled up with Mexican officials in moving illicit wheat across the border; the variety had not yet been released in Mexico for commercial use. The farmer agreed.

Staley arranged two semi-trailer grain trucks to be at the border to haul the seed wheat – Staley christened it MexiPak; the name stuck – to the port at Los Angeles. Staley rode along. They arrived at the port on a weekend. An American-flag carrier was scheduled to depart LA on Sunday evening with Karachi as one of its intended ports. But no dockworkers were there on the weekend. Staley called the President of the line and said, "We've got people starving in Pakistan; you must help us."

'Nuff said. The wheat was loaded onto the ship before it departed Sunday evening.

Meanwhile, Brookshier worked with Secretary A.A. Khan and his Agricultural Extension staff on a plan to get maximum multiplication of the seed. When the ship arrived at the Port of Karachi the wheat was off-loaded to a convoy of Pakistani Army trucks which fanned out across the fertile, irrigated Punjab of the Indus Valley and distributed the seed according to the plan. Cooperating farmers were each given a two-kilogram packet of seed with instructions on how to plant and tend it to get maximum multiplication. The seed multiplied manifold and was distributed widely.

The result helped verify Norm Borlaug's prediction. By the spring of 1968, primarily due to the Lerma Rojo variety, but supplemented with the new MexiPak, Pakistan's wheat production had reached an unprecedented eight million tons. Poor people in West Pakistan now had reasonably adequate diets. The crimson Lerma Rojo was the largest contributor initially to self-sufficiency, but within the next two or three years, because of taste preferences, the white MexiPak had largely replaced the red wheat.

In the spring of 1968, Leon learned that a prestigious entourage to include Norm Borlaug together with Lowell Hardin and Frosty Hill was expected to cross over to Lahore, Pakistan from India. Frosty Hill, Vice President of the Ford Foundation, was one of three people who had conceptualized the first international agricultural research center, the International Rice Research Institute (IRRI), located in the Philippines, that was commissioned in 1960. Lowell Hardin, then employed by the Ford Foundation, was one of the founding trustees of CIMMYT, which was commissioned in 1966 as the second in the soon-to-be-expanding set of international centers.

Florence and Leon jumped at the chance to open their house in the historic city of Lahore, where they had moved a year earlier from Karachi, to this distinguished group to introduce them to top-level Pakistani officials, including the colorful Minister of Agriculture, Khuda Baksh Bucha. The guests of honor reported that as they crossed the border from India, swarms of Pakistanis cheered the revered Norm Borlaug, who was rapidly becoming known as the Father of the Green Revolution.

In 1970, Norm Borlaug was awarded the Nobel Peace Prize for his pioneering work that led to the Green Revolution. The excitement of being a small player in such a dramatic event – helping relieve hunger for the masses – was exhilarating to Leon, to say the least.

Leon told Bill Kontos that for this, this, and this, he would agree to return for a second tour. With a broad smile, Bill said, "No problem!"

That's how close the Hessers came to going back to Kansas City where, Leon said, "I would have been bored to tears."

## Chapter Two

## Childhood Influences

Leon Hesser and Florence Ellen Life each grew up in a family that had lived within 10 miles of where their ancestors had settled in the wilderness three or four generations earlier, in conservative east central Indiana. What had influenced these two to become vagabonds?

The contrast between their childhood lives and their experiences in Pakistan and other foreign countries could hardly have been greater. Yet, once they overcame the initial shock of a new and different culture, they blossomed and flourished. Are they so unique that their style of life and its adventures cannot be duplicated by others, or are there lessons from their lives that others who are so inclined may draw upon?

Florence Life and Leon Hesser went from ordinary backgrounds to achieve extraordinary accomplishments. An implicit theme of this narrative is, "If they can do it, you can too." The challenge for those who are so inclined is to take pointers from the life experiences of this couple, explore some of the many exciting options the world has to offer, strike a course and reap the rewards of a fulfilling life.

Leon and Florence grew up in circumstances that were in some ways similar and in other ways quite different. Both were reared in families with religious values, families that espoused love, honesty, trustworthiness, and kindness. They each had one sibling of the opposite sex whom they loved and admired. Divorce was unthinkable in either family; both sets of parents were deeply devoted to their spouses.

Both fathers went to rural schools through the eighth grade, with little opportunity to go on to high school. Both mothers graduated from high school, Mrs. Life in a city school and Mrs. Hesser in one of the early rural consolidated schools in eastern Indiana.

Leon and Florence grew up in the depths of the Great Depression, though the two families fared a bit differently. The Hessers were rural people, farmers, who had plenty to eat but very little cash money. The Lifes were some 15 years older than the Hessers and since Mr. Life had worked steadily for two decades as a master machinist the family had a secure, steady income. During the Depression Mr. Life built a new, larger-than-the-average house in the county-seat town of Winchester, Indiana. The 12-room structure had four large pillars in front, inspired by the Life family's summer vacation visit to George Washington's Mount Vernon.

Leon's earliest remembrance was living with his parents and younger sister in a worked-over log house in the village of Lickskillet, a few miles from Winchester in east central Indiana. Lickskillet consisted of Miranda's grocery; Miller's garage; a lightly-used church held over from the nineteenth century with two entrance doors in front – one for the men and one for the women; and a dozen houses within walking distance of the grocery store, which doubled as the town hall. Men in the neighborhood sat around the wood-burning stove each evening and swapped stories.

The Hesser house no longer looked as though it were basically a log structure. It had been built onto, weather-boarded and fitted with a porch and swing in front. REMC had not yet brought electricity to the area, so they had a kerosene cook stove and kerosene lamps. All the neighbors had the same, with one exception: the Merandas had a Delco generator that provided electric power for lights for both the grocery store and their home next door. But the gasoline pump in front of the grocery store was still manually powered by Gail Meranda's moving a long lever back and forth as he watched to see when the gasoline reached the intended gallon-marker on the cylindrical glass container. He would then stop pumping and, by gravity, empty the contents through a hose into the customer's car or truck. At 15 cents a gallon during the Great Depression, not many customers said, "Fill 'er up!"

As a toddler, Leon was often allowed to roam outside in the well-fenced lawn to get fresh air and burn some of his excess energy. He doesn't remember this incident, but his parents reminded him later what a close call he had.

One fine day when he was 18 months old, as he was roaming the lawn he came up missing. After an agonizing search, when his parents were about to call in neighbors as additional scouts, they finally found him tromping around down in one of the two holes of the outside privy. His father confessed later that he thought it would have been easier to throw him away and make a new one than to clean him up, but his mother's good sense prevailed.

*Leon Hesser learning farm management principles*
*under the tutelage of his father, 1928*

In 1935, when Leon was 10, the family moved to a fairly large farm that Mr. Hesser had rented on a crop-share basis. Even before the move Leon's father had taught him to drive the family's 1929 Oldsmobile. After the move Leon drove the car twice a day, less than a mile each way, to feed the livestock at an alternate set of farm buildings. Father bought a new 1935 Model A John Deere tractor which Leon drove to prepare land for planting corn and soybeans while Father planted the crops with a two-row, horse-drawn planter. Father bought a John Deere tractor because it had a hand clutch, which Leon could activate. Most other makes of tractor had foot clutches; Leon was not yet heavy enough to activate a foot clutch. Nor was he strong enough to raise and lower the two-row corn cultivators on the John Deere Model A, so Father invested in an easy-to-manipulate hydraulic system.

Leon enjoyed working in the field, especially on the brand-new tractor; he took pride in helping achieve the family's goals on the farm. His father had spent much time with him, even before they moved to the new farm, teaching him how to care for the pigs, cows and chickens. At the new farm they expanded their livestock holdings to include a stable of draft horses and a flock of sheep. There were plenty of chores to do. In those days no one in rural areas ever thought about "child labor" in a negative way. Since pioneer days, farm boys were expected to share the workload from an early age, and mostly the lads were happy to contribute to the family's welfare.

Even after they moved to the new farm, the Hessers continued to attend the church in Lickskillet. Sunday School was held every Sunday morning; a self-ordained preacher held church services on alternate Sundays. On Easter Sunday and at the Christmas service there might be as many as 20 in the congregation; most other times, fewer. When Leon was 12 he was baptized by emersion in near-by White River which, although it was muddy from the spring rains, cleansed his soul of any lingering sins. (He had quit smoking when he was seven; he got caught smoking corn silks behind the barn!)

When Leon was 15 the congregation chose him to be the Sunday School Superintendent, which required that he stand in the front of the sanctuary and announce that classes would begin right after they all sang a song to the accompaniment of Edith Yost, who managed with one finger on the antique piano to keep them reasonably well in tune. Following the classes Leon would ask Deacon Jones or dear old Mrs. Cook to say a prayer to dismiss the congregation. When he was 18, Leon was elected president of the county-wide Christian Youth Congress; this position was cut short by his being called to duty in World War II.

Leon's Christian heritage stemmed mostly from his mother's side, whose parents were influenced heavily in their religious beliefs by Great Grandma Acenath Smith Edwards, who descended from a long line of Quakers. Leon knew Great Grandma Acenath; he was seven when she died at age 94. She spoke in "thees" and "thous." She was a wonderful storyteller and frequently told Leon about her childhood days in the Indiana wilderness at mid-19th century. Both the Smiths and the Edwardses, whose ancestors had emigrated from the British Isles in the 17th and 18th centuries, were early pioneers in eastern Indiana, having come up from North Carolina to escape the plight of slavery.

Leon attended Lincoln School for 12 years, the same rural consolidated school from which his mother had graduated in 1919. There were 15 in his graduating class; nine had been together all 12 years. As if to predict his future leadership role in agricultural development, the editor of the 1943 Lincoln High School *Yearbook* foresaw Leon as "the person most likely to be the first American farmer to spread manure with an airplane."

Lincoln School had no gymnasium; the boys on the basketball team practiced during recess on a cinder-floored outdoor court. Twice a week, the team was transported six miles by school bus to a real gym for practice. Even with this handicap, the team always did well in competition with other county teams.

Leon took courses in Vocational Agriculture at Lincoln High and from the age of 10 he participated in 4-H with chickens and pigs. By the time he was 18, he had sufficient knowledge about farming and farm management that he could have confidently operated his own farm business, although he would undoubtedly have conferred with his father before making major decisions. In fact, when he was 18, he made an agreement with a neighboring landowner to farm some of his land on a share basis. But, greetings from Uncle Sam changed that.

Florence was born to middle-age parents: Chester Christian Life and LaNella Ann Bavender.

She says, "When reflecting on my childhood, a few descriptive words capture my emotions: happy, lonely, loved, disciplined." The combined backgrounds of her parents contributed to Florence's philosophy of life.

Florence's father was the child of a Billy Sunday-type minister. During the late nineteenth century, the Reverend Life held revivals all over Indiana, leaving the farming to the boys. Florence's father, the eldest of nine children, grew up doing much of the planting and harvesting on the farm and was responsible for the daily care of the farm animals. All of his life he felt responsible for his brothers and sisters. From a very early age he showed mechanical ability – no doubt from his German heritage.

Florence's mother carried an embarrassing burden: her father, Hugh Bavender, was an alcoholic – known as the "town drunk." He and his bride, Mary Ellen Zachery, had been victims of the Civil War. Hugh was too young for the war, but his brother was crippled so badly that Hugh didn't recognize him when he came hobbling home. Mary Ellen's well-to-do parents had servants before the war – Mary Ellen had never even tied her shoes herself before she was married. After the war, the young couple migrated to Indiana, where Hugh was able to get day labor. Mary Ellen was never happy in the new environment. She eventually received a small inheritance, but the family wealth had largely dissipated along with the security and culture she had enjoyed as a child.

*Eight-year-old Florence beside Mother,*
*Auntie Scheltneck and Father Life*

Dr. and Mrs. Scheltneck, who lived across the street from Florence's mother when she was a girl, took an interest in her and essentially raised her during her high school years. Auntie Scheltneck taught Nellie many things: sewing, making a home, and cooking. This gave her a self-image she could not have had from her own parents, who were living from hand to mouth most of the time. It made her appreciate education; her great pride was having graduated from Hagerstown High School, in 1904. She also won a prize – several yards of fine material for a dress – for being the most popular girl in town.

Florence's parents had been married ten years when her brother Hugh Jacob was born. Florence came along seven years later. Jake was out and gone shortly after Florence started to school, so she essentially led the life of an only child.

Florence says, "I never in my life doubted that I was loved, even though I was certainly an accident; who would purposely have a second child after seven years – at age 43?"

"One of my fondest memories," said Florence, "is of Mother reading to me of an afternoon, seated in a rocker by the furnace's register. Mother loved books; she helped establish the first little library in Redkey, Indiana where my parents resided until I was eleven. Bathed, combed and dressed up, we would walk the five or six blocks to the fire station and unlock the tiny library in a backroom. I loved to read the many books while seated in a corner as mother and her friends stocked the shelves and catalogued the books."

After the family moved to Winchester when Florence was eleven, she and her friend Betty Jean walked to a much larger library three or four times a week. With little else to do, they read most of the novels. Florence says, "I especially loved Jean Stratton Porter, partly because her birthday was the same day as mine."

Florence's mother was a close friend of Emma Meyer, the trusted house-keeper at the home of James Goodrich, a former Governor of Indiana. The mansion was just around the corner from the Life's home on High Street in Winchester. Governor Goodrich had a large, well-stocked library. When Miss Meyer entertained The Sunshine Club at the mansion, Florence would slip into the library and look at the books, hoping someday to be able to sit there and read for awhile. Or better still, have her own library.

Florence's mother refused to have a big family. She felt that people who "multiplied like flies" were not well advised. She was an advocate of women taking responsibility for their lives – she would have been a great abortionist. She was profoundly against drink and was an active member of the Women's Christian Temperance Union (WCTU) undoubtedly because of her father's problem. She did not allow brother and sister to speak harshly to one another – she simply did not tolerate verbal abuse.

"She was the disciplinarian in the family, calling Dad in to assist only when my brother and I appeared not to be listening to her."

In the family routine everyone was up at 7 a.m. Florence was always expected to eat breakfast, then go to church or school, be there on time, and "when there I must remember who I am and do unto others as I would have them do unto me." This included doing well in school. Father encouraged her to write and showed her how to form letters. He also helped her with math. On a blackboard she learned to write her name before she started school. She was to please her parents and not embarrass them.

"So, that one time when I was spanked in the first grade I didn't tell my parents – ever!"

One of the things Florence enjoyed as a girl was dressing up. Between her ages of five to fourteen, her mother purchased lovely clothes from a rich little girl who was two or three years older. It was a gift that helped give Florence a sound self-image.

Florence's parents traveled on extended vacations even when the Depression hung over Indiana. In 1934 when she was nine her folks took her to the Chicago World's Fair. In 1935, when Florence was 10 and her brother was 18, the family went to the East coast – a life-influencing venture – in an old Willys Knight, a rather large, black four-door sedan. Father Life knew motors, so he could "get out and get under" if anything went wrong.

Florence's grade-school years were occupied with 4-H. She took sewing and won ribbons with her dress two years in a row, a reassuring experience. Her mother coached her with the sewing.

Florence says, "I enjoyed modeling the dress each year; this, too, gave me confidence in teenage self."

Florence says, "I was proud of my academic and social standing in high school and separated myself from kids who came from homes filled with drink and abuse."

One of the things that influenced Florence's value system was her mother's returning each year to her high-school alumni banquet, for which she had to have a new outfit and hair-do; this required meticulous preparations prior to the banquet. She lived to go back to Hagerstown and show her classmates how well she had done. Her hats and gloves spawned many comments. She was a model of a lady.

Reflecting her mother's example, Florence took pride in knowing who she was. She also took pride in her own graduation and in the clothes her mother and dad bought for her. This gave her a feeling of confidence and independence.

Attending the local Methodist church was part of the Life family's weekly routine. One of Florence's greatest influences was Reverend Herbert Boase, the pastor for about ten years – a dear man who was born in England and educated in the States with a doctor's degree in theology. He was well informed and met with a group of four or five girls every Sunday afternoon from four to six. During this time of Youth Fellowship he taught many things, including how to think independently. He was informed and concerned about the upcoming war with Germany; the girls absorbed his geography, history and philosophy. He provided an understanding of the church's beliefs and re-enforced the value systems that were extant in the girls' homes.

Florence's dad remodeled or rebuilt every home her parents owned. In a day when most housing in the Midwest was not modern, he installed furnaces, bathrooms and extra rooms, all in his spare time. His last house was completed when Florence was thirteen; he rebuilt an older house into a twelve-room home with a small apartment in the back which furnished income for Florence's mother after he was gone.

The neighborhood was safe, day and night. The front door was seldom locked. But, Florence says in many ways her parents were overly protective. For example, her mother would not allow her to baby-sit; she would get enough of that when she had children of her own. Most of all, "they did not want me to marry too young or marry a farmer; life on a farm would be too difficult for me, a city girl."

## Chapter Three

## The War Years

Leon turned his head for one last glance as he left the personnel office of the local Anchor Hocking glass factory. His fleeting look was met by an electrifying smile from the attractive young lady who had processed his termination-of-employment papers. He had completed a three-month stint at the factory that winter and was returning to the farm to help his father plant corn and soybeans. It was midday on a Friday in early March of 1944 – the middle of World War II.

Saturday nights in the little town of Winchester, Indiana, were special. Country folks who had put in long hours during the week quit early on Saturday and went to town to do their weekly shopping, but mostly to walk the town square and visit friends. Young people alternated between walking the square, boys trailing giggling girls, and – if they had enough change to buy a Coke – stopping at the only respectable dig at the time: the Rainbow Restaurant.

Leon had plenty of change. At 40 cents an hour he had earned $16 a week, less federal and state income taxes and Franklin Roosevelt's brand-new Social Security tax, at the factory that winter. As he entered the Rainbow that Saturday night, the very next day after terminating at the factory, he was hailed to one of the booths.

"Hello, Leon. I'm Florence. May I introduce you to my friend Alice?" Leon was charmed by Florence's friendly manner, her warm personality, her genuine smile.

When Leon mentioned sometime later that he was surprised she had remembered his name, she said, "I not only knew your name, I knew your whole history," from the personnel files at the office.

The next day, Sunday afternoon, Leon and a high-school buddy Cliff went to the Rainbow to indulge in another Coke. Guess who? She was standing, this time, with her friend Melba. Leon judged her come-hither smile to be an invitation to chat and started edging in her direction when – oops – she dropped her handkerchief. (She swears to this day it was accidental!) Slightly embarrassed, Leon picked it up and with a half-grin handed it to her. The ensuing conversation led to a double date that night.

*Farm boy and city girl fall madly in love*

As they walked home to get ready for the evening, Melba told Florence she would not go because she knew a family of garbage collectors with the same surname as Cliff's.

Florence said, "You *are* going! Mother would never let me go alone on a date with a farm boy."

Melba finally agreed that they would call and ask Marceil, a country girl whom they reckoned would know the boys. If Marceil said the boys were respectable, she would agree to go.

Marceil said, "Oh, they are fine boys." The girls didn't know until weeks afterward that Marceil was Leon's first cousin.

Despite the scarcity of gasoline – Cliff had only a "B" ration card for his 1934 Ford roadster – the foursome ventured out of town to a movie.

They went 10 miles east to Union City! Melba had a horrible time; it turned out that Cliff's arms were a bit too long. The other two hit it off beautifully. But Leon, in his rural naiveté, neither kissed Florence goodnight nor asked for another date when he took her to the door. As a consequence he had to call six times before she agreed to a second date.

Meanwhile, Leon – a healthy 18-year-old – received "Greetings" from Uncle Sam. Florence and Leon had only occasional dates during March and April, but during May and early June they were together constantly, met each others' parents and – you guessed it – fell deeply in love.

After passing the Army's physical, Leon reported to Fort Benjamin Harrison at Indianapolis on June 10 and a few days later was sent for basic training at Camp Hood, Texas. His barracks consisted of about 30 young

*Bunkmate Hugh Hefner signs Leon's autograph book, 1944*

men whose names all started with "H:" Hirsch, Hise, Hesser, Hefner, Heavner, Hill, etc. Leon's bunkmate – they were a couple of 18-year-olds – was Hugh Hefner. At that time, Hugh was just one of the boys – he put his pants on one leg at a time, just like all the others.

But even at that time, Hugh demonstrated differences from the others. For example, near the end of the 17-week basic training, when Leon asked each of his barracks-mates to write a remembrance in his autograph book, most of them jotted down a few words: "God bless you as a soldier, and to Flossie and you the happiest life in the world," or "We have been swell buddies . . . May you & Florence have the best of everything."

Hugh's entry was unique. The group had just accomplished its final 20-mile march with full field pack. Hugh exhibited artistic ability when he did a caricature, which he signed "Hef."

Between June 10, 1944 and June 10, 1946 Florence and Leon saw each other only during his 10-day furlough in November, between basic training and his departure for overseas. During that time, in an effort to get better acquainted with her farmer-turned-soldier friend, Florence's father invited Leon to the offices of the Life Manufacturing Company for a chat.

In the ensuing conversation, Leon told Mr. Life that he was very much in love with his daughter and pleaded for his consent to marry her after the war. Following the session, Mr. Life gave a crisp assessment to Mrs. Life, who had higher expectations for a son-in-law than a farm boy: "Well, one thing's for sure, Leon is no bullshitter!" Coming from father Life, that was indeed a compliment.

Mr. Life gave his consent. For the engagement ring, Leon invested about two months' salary as a Private in the United States Army. Florence's sister-in-law squinted to see the diamond as she said "Isn't it cute!"

They were together constantly, and passionately, during those ten days. Yet, strange as it may seem to young people today, she remained a virgin when he gave her that last good-bye kiss before boarding a train for the California port of embarkation. He was sent to the Pacific on the Liberty ship *USS General Robert L. Howze* along with 3,499 other sad sacks. During the 34-day trip to their destination they crossed the equator on Christmas Eve.

Florence wrote to Leon almost every day during his time overseas and Leon wrote as often as he could, about once each week. Against all rules, Leon had given Florence a code before he left: if he signed at the end of a letter simply the words, 'Love, Leon' she was to take the first letter of each paragraph to spell the location where he was at the time. The code in his first communication after he reached his destination spelled L E Y T E.

General MacArthur had taken Leyte in his triumphant return to the Philippines, but with heavy casualties. Leon was one of the many replacements to join the forces before their move to the northernmost island of Luzon in an attempt to liberate Manila. He was assigned to G Company, 2nd Battalion, 34th Regiment, 24th Division. The pink-skinned tenderfoot replacements – many, like Leon, still teenagers – were eyed with skepticism by the rough and ragged survivors of Leyte, but they would have to do.

The huge convoy approached the western coast of Luzon on the evening of January 28, 1945. The ships' guns bombarded the coast all that night. The next morning the guns silenced while the troops made a successful beachhead. There were no casualties, for the enemy had retreated – leaving a trail of burning bridges – to well-fortified positions in the rugged hills several miles inland in Zigzag Pass. The military objective was to clear Route # 7, which as the name implies, ran in zigzag fashion through the pass. The jagged corners, replete with machinegun nests, were an infantryman's nightmare.

The U.S. Army's intelligence had suggested that there were only a few Japanese soldiers in the pass and that they were not well supplied with arsenal.

Wrong! In the ensuing action, G Company made a flanking reconnaissance, with few casualties. In late afternoon they began to dig in for the night on the side of a slope. Unnoticed as yet, an enemy soldier with a walkie-talkie, perched high in a tall tree, radioed G Company's position to his mortar company. The next several minutes – it seemed like hours – were literal Hell.

Alternately, Leon buried his face in the ground and prayed, then jumped up and ran for a safer spot. It seemed that each time he ran, a shell exploded where he had been lying. He says, "I'll never doubt that God held my hand." When the shelling ended, those who were able helped carry the less fortunate over a long, rugged trail to awaiting ambulances.

After three days of taking a beating in Zigzag, the commander pulled the troops back a few miles to make camp and regroup. Among others in Leon's squad of 10 soldiers, the BAR (Browning Automatic Rifle) man had been killed.

While in camp the squad leader said, "Hesser, you look strong. We'll give you the BAR." Obediently, Leon took the imposing thing to a makeshift range and fired a few rounds to get a feel for it.

As he returned to camp a jeep carrying Captain Fremont P. Koch, MD pulled up. He said, "Is your name Hesser?"

"Yes, sir."

"How would you like to transfer to the Medics?"

"Sir, anything is better than carrying this BAR!"

Captain Koch did not tell Leon at the time, but he learned later that the 34th had lost 12 Medics when an artillery shell landed in the Second Battalion Aid Station, so they transferred a dozen of the new recruits to replace them. Leon finished out the war in the Medics, being one of the few who has ever earned both the Combat Infantry Badge and the Combat Medics Badge.

Leon recalls, "One sad event during the remainder of the war was my writing out the tag of a contemporary who had been given my BAR: 'KIA.' By that time, we were 19."

During mail call at camp, Leon had several letters from Florence. He also had a letter from his mother.

She wrote, "Son, if you can get your hands on a Bible, you might find comfort in reading the 91st Psalm."

Leon checked around but could find no one who was carrying a Bible. Several had New Testaments – Leon's, in his left breast pocket, had a brass cover intended to slow a bullet aimed at his heart – but no one had a Bible.

As Sunday approached, the Regimental Chaplain announced that he would hold services in an adjoining coconut grove. Filipinos had placed a series of coconut logs in parallel fashion to serve as pews. Attendance was exceptionally good that Sunday morning – standing room only!

The Chaplain stood before the troops at a makeshift alter and pulpit and said, "For my text this morning, I'm taking the 91st Psalm."

Leon says, "I knew my mother was tuned in, but I hadn't realized before that she had a hot line."

The Chaplain proceeded:

*He who dwells in the shelter of the Most High, who abides in the shadow of the Almighty, will say to the Lord, 'My refuge and my fortress; my God, in whom I trust.'*

*For he will deliver you from the snare of the fowler and from the deadly pestilence; he will cover you with his pinions, and under his wings you will find refuge; his faithfulness is a shield and buckler.*

*You will not fear the terror of the night, nor the arrow that flies by day, nor the pestilence that stalks in darkness, nor the destruction that wastes at noonday.*

*A thousand may fall at your side, ten thousand at your right hand; but it will not come near you. . . . For he will give his angels charge of you to guard you in all your ways.*

After Luzon came mopping-up operations on the island of Mindoro, toward the middle of the Philippines, and then on the southernmost island of Mindanao. While they were on Mindoro, in April 1945, President Roosevelt died. While on Mindanao, President Truman gave the order in August to drop the Atomic bomb on Hiroshima. Two months later Leon sailed to Japan as part of the Army of Occupation.

By early May 1946 Leon had been promoted twice and had acquired enough points to return to the States to be discharged. While waiting to board ship, in the same barracks room with 14 other Staff Sergeants, one of his roommates broke out with an obvious case of the chicken pox.

Leon says, "I recommended that the guy cover his face as best he could and proceed to get on the ship, but the better judgment of the others prevailed; the sad sack went drooping off to sick bay and all 15 of us were summarily quarantined for three weeks! One of the mathematical geniuses in the group calculated that if we each came down consecutively with the malady, we would be in quarantine for three and a half years!" Fortunately, none did.

Meanwhile, for three long weeks Florence anticipated a phone call from Leon saying he had arrived in the States. International phone calls at that time were beyond the financial means of a mere GI Joe.

The call finally came from Seattle: "I'll be home in 10 days!" Neighbors subsequently reported that Leon literally ran the six blocks from the bus station to Florence's home at 407 High Street, carrying a duffle bag with his entire earthly possessions.

One must look hard to find something good that stems from such a catastrophic event as World War II. In Leon's case, and undoubtedly for many others, being exposed to how people live in other parts of the world was both educational and stimulating. Leon was introduced to native peoples of the Philippines during the war and then to the Japanese during the Army of Occupation. After having been raised on a farm in the Midwest he was fascinated by the vastly different agricultural systems as well as the cultures in those lands.

When the war ended, Capt. Koch asked Leon what he planned to do when he returned to the States. Shortly after Leon had joined his unit, Capt. Koch asked him to be his clerk, which amounted to trailing him during sick call and writing the diagnoses as he dictated them. That took Leon from a Private First Class to a Corporal. Soon, he was promoted to Sergeant and, by the time he turned 20, to Staff Sergeant in charge of administering the Aid Station.

Leon told Capt. Koch that he and Florence planned to get married soon after he was discharged from the Army and more than likely he would operate his own farm business. Capt. Koch told Leon he should consider going to college. He said he could get him admitted to Dartmouth, his alma mater, that it would cost about $6,000 total for the four years and he would lend Leon the money.

Leon recalls, "I think this was the first time anyone had seriously suggested that I should go to college. It seemed such a strange idea to me that I politely declined his offer."

But Capt. Koch's question got Leon to thinking about college. While he was in Japan with the Army of Occupation he asked his parents to see if they could get him admitted to Purdue University. He was accepted subject to finding housing. Housing for married couples was extremely tight on campus because many ex-GIs were going to college. They finally found a place about 25 miles from campus. When they announced this to Florence's parents, they said in effect, "If you two get married and go to college you will starve to death."

The two were unwavering in their desire to get married, and they did. Leon recalls thinking, *Maybe the parents are right; maybe it would be unreasonable for us to try to go to college.*

## Chapter Four

## Marriage, Farm and Family

During the 18 months of courtship by mail from halfway 'round the world, Florence and Leon *dreamed* of the day when they would be together again. Time dragged. Their love for each other grew stronger and stronger; the anticipation of their being together again was overwhelming. Florence rushed outside to meet Leon when old Mrs. Mamie Davis, a neighbor across the street from the Life's, called Florence to say, "There's a soldier running up the street with a duffle bag; is he yours?"

There had never been any doubt in either of their minds that they were meant for each other. They would waste no time in getting married.

Meanwhile, Leon had a few administrative things to take care of. One was officially to record his discharge from the Army. To accomplish that he went to the courthouse to see Merritt Monks, Randolph County Recorder and a man well known to Leon because he had been a prominent referee of high school basketball games when Leon was playing. Merritt said, "Leon, while you're here, why don't you register to vote?"

Leon said, "Merritt, I'm not old enough yet to vote."

In a thundering voice that could be heard all over the courthouse Merritt said, "Now isn't *that* a Hell of a note – been away for two years fighting in the war and still not old enough to vote!"

Leon also needed to get reacquainted with his family – his parents and his sister, Vivian, his only sibling. Early in that reunion, Leon's mother said when the two were alone, "You are not going to get married right away are you?"

*Leon Hesser and Florence Life*
*Bride and Groom, August 11, 1946*

With a straight face Leon said, "No, of course not; we're going to wait until I'm 21!" That would be in July, the next month. Seeing that it was inevitable, and perhaps to secure a few more days at home for her hero son, she suggested that the wedding be on her birthday, which was Sunday, August 11. Everyone agreed. Florence planned a late-afternoon wedding to be held in the local Methodist Church.

Sunday, August 11, turned out to be the hottest day of the year in Winchester, Indiana. The church was packed with friends and family from both sides. And that was before the church was air-conditioned. Florence had been to a friend's wedding several days earlier in which guests continued arriving after the ceremony had started. That would not happen in *her* wedding. She indicated in the invitations that the wedding would be at 6 p.m., but actually delayed the ceremony until 30 minutes later. Everyone was on time according to the invitation, which meant they sweltered in the heat for 30 minutes before the ceremony started. Meanwhile, some wondered whether Leon might have had second thoughts!

Other than that it was a beautiful ceremony. Reverend Boase officiated. Florence had asked Leon's sister, Vivian, to be Maid of Honor and three of her close friends to be Bridesmaids. Leon asked his cousin, Wayne McGuire, to be Best Man plus two cousins and a schoolmate to be Groomsmen.

The bride and groom took a week for their honeymoon, crossing into Canada at Detroit then proceeding to Niagara Falls. They spent six days getting to Niagara Falls, which left only one day to get back to Winchester in time to go to work Monday morning. Several people back home suggested to the bride and groom that they must have especially enjoyed the fabulous lighting on Niagara Falls at night. Sheepishly, Leon had to say, "We didn't see the lighting at the Falls; they didn't turn the lights on until 9 o'clock."

Father Life had secretly vowed to transform Leon into a Methodist, tool-maker and Democrat. In the first of the trilogy – via marriage to his only daughter – he had succeeded. In an attempt at the second he got Leon a job as an apprentice toolmaker at locally owned Kelly Tool Company, where he worked for about one year at 60 cents an hour plus a GI-bill stipend. The precision of the tool work – studying blueprints and running lathes and milling machines – was interesting for a while, but Florence soon recognized that Leon was becoming dissatisfied – the shop was too confining.

At about that time Leon's father told him of a farm next to his – the Heaston place, one of the better farms in the county – that was coming up for rent.

Leon says, "Based largely on my father's reputation as a farmer, dear old Mrs. Heaston gave me a good deal. Florence and I lived there for five years while I operated the farm."

By being that close to his father's farm, they could exchange equipment and work together in the fields. Father agreed that a used tractor and plow were about the only major items of equipment that Leon would need to buy; Father had a full line of equipment that they could share.

Florence continued to work in town so they could buy groceries, until Gwendolyn was born during the second year on the farm.

The long-awaited birth was accompanied by shock. It was a difficult birth that, in retrospect, should have been by cesarean section. It was further complicated by the young doctor's having in the middle of the night prescribed a shot to delay the process until morning.

Whether due to the use of instruments during the difficult delivery, or to complications from the longer than natural delay in delivery, baby Gwendolyn suffered a brain injury.

One doctor suggested that the child might have to be institutionalized. Florence and Leon were adamantly against that; they would give her every advantage they could in their own home. That turned out to have been a wise decision.

With love and patience, Gwendolyn continued to grow intellectually, though with more difficulty and slower than her peers. Ultimately, she married and presented the grandparents with a beautiful and vivacious granddaughter.

After five years on the farm the Hessers were well integrated into the community: they joined Rural Youth; Leon was a member of the Jaycees; they served as youth counselors at the Methodist Church; Florence helped take the Census. They were also doing well as young farmers. They had paid for a new tractor outfit and acquired several other items of equipment. But they had to move when Mrs. Heaston died.

When Reed Abel, President of the local Randolph County Bank and an influential businessman, learned that the Hessers would have to move he approached Leon to say he had a farm in the southern part of the county he would like Leon to operate. They worked out a deal.

Mr. Abel remodeled the barn to Leon's specifications and the house to Florence's. In the new neighborhood they joined the small, rural Methodist Church and quickly became friends with a number of other young people in the community.

At the time, the local public school had no kindergarten. Partly because she was anxious for Gwen to experience structured learning with other children, Florence took the lead in organizing a kindergarten to be held in a new Community Center next to the Methodist Church. It was well accepted and supported by the community and was eventually integrated into the public school system.

In the wee hours of morning on January 25, 1954, George Christian was born. Leon had to borrow a nickel from a nurse at the hospital to call Mrs.

*Gwen Hesser adoring her little brother, George*

Life and say, "It's a boy, and he's a dandy!" The new baby was named after his two grandfathers: George was Leon's father's name; Christian was the first or second name of each of a long line of ancestors in the Life family.

They lived on and operated Abel Acres for three years. Leon says, "I view our time at Abel Acres as one in which I was transformed from being George Hesser's son to being Mr. Leon Hesser. In many ways, our life was ideal; we were respected in the community and had made many friends – but something was missing."

Florence recalls, "During the early planning phases of the new farm operation, Leon was content. But it soon became routine and I sensed that he was becoming bored."

In the spring of 1955, the third year on Abel Acres, Leon found on his luncheon plate when he came in from the field a magazine that was opened to an article about a young couple in their late 20s with two children in which the father was attending the University of Georgia. Florence said, "If he can do it, you can too."

That was a life-altering moment for the Hesser family.

## Chapter Five

## Juggling Studies, Work and Children at Purdue

The first day it rained enough to keep Leon out of the field he and Florence drove to Lafayette, surveyed the Purdue campus and he met with Dean Pfendler, Dean of Students. Leon told him his background and asked, "Would it be crazy for a 30-year-old man who has been too busy on the farm to read a book to try to make it at the University?"

The Dean asked Leon several questions. Finally he said, "What does your wife think about this?"

With glee Leon said, "It was her idea!"

With that, Dean Pfendler leaned forward, looked at Leon over the rim of his glasses, and said, "Young man, all I will do is encourage you." That was all Leon needed. He sold his farm possessions at an auction sale in August and entered Purdue as a freshman in September.

Leon had several misgivings during the summer. More than one neighbor said he was crazy to give up such an opportunity as he had on Abel Acres; furthermore, in competing with kids just out of high school, "You will flunk out by Christmas."

Leon's father had a hard time trying to comprehend the decision, but remained silent. His mother said she thought he was working too hard on the farm; it was a good decision. Mr. Abel expressed disappointment that Leon and Florence would be leaving his farm, but as a former schoolteacher he knew the importance of a good education so he congratulated them and gave his blessing.

Leon recalls thinking, *What if I do flunk out by Christmas? What will we do then? I am sure to flunk chemistry, because Lincoln High didn't have a chemistry lab and didn't even offer chemistry.*

From a neighbor who had graduated from Purdue, Leon borrowed a chemistry book. During the summer he studied the book one page at a time during brief intervals as the cows were being milked with the Surge milking machine. That paid off handsomely.

Leon made straight "A"s in chemistry while several kids flunked even though they had had chemistry in high school.

Leon says, "My approach was to memorize formulas before each class, though I confess I soon forgot them. I remember one incident in particular. The professor asked at the beginning of a session, 'Who can tell me how to make gasoline?' I held up my hand; no one else did.

"When he called on me I said, 'You can make gasoline by the catalytic hydrogenation of dimerized isobutalene.' All the others in the class stared at me as if to say, 'Who's that old sonovabitch?'"

Florence and Leon drove to Lafayette during the summer before he entered Purdue so he could take the entrance exams. As one of the tests Leon was asked to write a short two-page story about something he had done in his youth.

He wrote about his experience with a 4-H pig project. A few weeks later he received a letter saying based on his tests and the story he had written he would be placed in English Composition 103 rather than English Composition 101.

If he were to make an "A" or a "B" in the class, he would get six hours credit rather than three. Leon said he was sure that someone had made a mistake, because about the only thing he had written during his farm days were checks and some of them bounced.

On the first day of class in Comp 103 the professor said, "Some of you in here are misplaced and it won't take me long to find out which ones."

With that, Leon was tempted to raise his hand and say, "Never mind, Sir, I'll save you the trouble; I'll leave now."

However, Leon says, with pure luck and the good graces of Professor Rowen, he got an "A" in the class. He attributes this to the excellent English grammar teachers at Lincoln School who "drilled us no end in diagramming sentences and formulating paragraphs."

Shortly after the Hessers arrived at the Purdue campus for Leon to begin his studies, Leon was asked to attend freshman orientation in the large auditorium of the new Stewart Music Hall. Florence and the two children went along. When they entered the auditorium to be seated, an usher said to Leon, "Parents are to go upstairs."

Leon said, "I'm a freshman, Bub!"

The usher shook his head and replied, "You never can tell these days."

A few minutes later the master of ceremonies in his introductory remarks said something like, "This new Music Hall has one of the largest auditoriums of its kind in the United States. It has the capacity to seat 6,328 people."

As he paused momentarily before proceeding to the next statement, 18-month-old George proclaimed loudly, "Ha, ha, ha!" It nearly broke up the audience.

During the first two years at Purdue Leon worked 20 hours a week at a Kroger grocery store. Florence had a good job as personal Secretary to the owner of a plumbing company, even though as she told him she wouldn't know a nipple from an elbow.

Daughter Gwen was in the first grade and 18-month-old son George was enrolled in a lovely pre-school. The Hessers lived comfortably in the university's old World War II Army barracks which ten years after the war were filled with married students, most with children. The conventional wisdom: There is nothing quite so permanent as a temporary building on a college campus!

Leon was asked many times why he had decided to quit farming and go back to school when he apparently had such a good start on the farm. His standard answer was that it was indeed a complex decision; many factors had to be considered.

But, he would say, "Probably the main reason was that I had married a city girl; she used to say the only thing she liked about farming was rainy days. Then, she would say, we either went to town or went to bed and I liked to do both."

During the first semester at Purdue Leon decided to try to finish the bachelor's degree in less than the normal four years and worked out a schedule to accomplish that if the Dean would OK it.

In a conference with Dean Pfendler in which Leon sought permission to take an overload the next semester, the Dean inquired about Leon's interests. Leon told him he was interested in the agriculture of other countries.

The Dean mentioned that the Foreign Agricultural Service of the U.S. Department of Agriculture placed agricultural attaches in U.S. embassies in many countries. Based on that, Leon did some research and wrote a term paper in Comp 103 on Public Law 480 – Food for Peace – which is administered by the FAS. His interest in foreign agriculture was growing.

By taking an overload – Leon took 23 credit hours each of the last four semesters – he was able to complete the bachelor's degree in three years. At a departmental ceremony during his last semester, Leon says he was both surprised and overjoyed to be given an award for having the highest scholastic index among graduating seniors in Agricultural Economics. Florence and his professors insisted that he should go on for a master's degree.

The decision to do so had been made easier when, based on a Civil Service examination that he had taken, he was appointed as a research assistant for the Economic Research Service, U.S. Department of Agriculture, while stationed at Purdue. Supervisors said if he would stay on he could work an irregular 40-hour week, take six hours of classes each semester, and write his thesis based on research he would do for the ERS. What a deal! The starting salary was $4,040 per year, much better than a conventional research assistantship.

During the entire time at Purdue, Leon and Florence made friends with many foreign students. Samir Asmar from Jordan was one example. Sam was handsome and gregarious. Girls flocked around him. He often came to the Hessers' barracks apartment to study and have meals.

Leon lost track of Sam after he graduated and Sam had no idea what Leon was doing. Twenty years later, while Leon was having coffee and a donut at the cafeteria in the offices of the International Fund for Agricultural Development in Rome, Sam spotted Leon as he came in the door – shouted, **Leon** – and came rushing over and gave him a big hug.

After catching up on each other's lives, Sam insisted that Leon join a team that he was putting together to do an agricultural assessment in Jordan. Leon agreed.

About the time Leon finished his master's degree, Dr. Lowell S. Hardin, Head of Purdue's Department of Agricultural Economics, was asked by the

Foreign Agricultural Service to go to Japan for three months during the summer of 1960 to evaluate the effectiveness of the Public Law 480 Food-for-Peace program. Knowing of Leon's interest in foreign agriculture and that he had been in Japan during the Occupation, Professor Hardin asked Leon to join him as research assistant. Leon was elated. Both wives went along and they had a ball.

*Florence and Leon (right) in Japan with*
*Professor Lowell and Mary Hardin, 1960*

As one of their duties, Lowell and Leon were invited one night to a geisha party. They had only small amounts of saki, but it was enough that their wives who were on the second storey heard them giggling as they came in the front door of International House.

When they got to the room, Lowell's wife Mary said, "Tell us about the party – was it suggestive?"

Lowell said, "Oh, no. One of the girls said, 'Tell me about ag-ri-cul-tur-al ec-o-nom-ics.'"

Mary, who had never been known to swear, shouted, "Oh, Hell!" That summer was the beginning of a very close, life-long friendship between the Hessers and the Hardins.

As Leon neared completion of the master's degree, professors encouraged him to continue toward a doctorate. Florence strongly urged him to get a Ph.D. Leon was enjoying life as a graduate student – it was much more fun than farming! But he told Florence he would not go beyond a master's degree unless she went to college.

Leon says, "She was more than my equal intellectually, but I was afraid we might grow apart if I were to get a Ph.D. while she had no college."

They discussed this issue several times with the same result. She insisted that it was not necessary for her to go to college, but that Leon must get a Ph.D.

During the summer of 1959, while Leon was still working on his master's degree, he and Florence went to the annual meeting of the American Farm Economics Association at Cornell. Leon interviewed and discussed alternatives with several people, including a representative of the Foreign Agricultural Service. Leon asked what advantage a doctorate might have for employment in the FAS.

She said it was not important at all – only those at the very top of the Service had doctorates. When Leon relayed that to John Mellor, a young professor of agricultural economics at Cornell with a strong interest in international agriculture, he laughed and said, "Sure, only if you want to get to the top!"

While at the Cornell meetings, Florence and Leon enjoyed a picnic lunch on one of the beautiful hills surrounding the university. The subject came up once again. She said, "You must get your Ph.D."

Leon said, "I will *not* go for a doctorate unless you go to college."

She hung her head in meditation. Then, she said, "I don't think I'm smart enough."

Leon retorted immediately, "You are right; you are not smart enough!"

Florence's eyes snapped! The next month she was a freshman at age 35 in the School of Science and Humanities at Purdue. She got her BA in the same ceremony in which Leon got his Ph.D. Purdue also awarded Florence a PHT: Putting Hubby Through. She ultimately earned an Ed.D, a doctorate in education.

## Chapter Six

## Kansas City: A Time of Seasoning

During their last year at Purdue, the Hessers wrestled with what they would do after graduation. Leon let it be known that he was interested in foreign work. He and Florence finally narrowed the possibilities down to two: a two-year stint in Chile with the Organization of American States, or a more permanent position in the Research Department of the Federal Reserve Bank of Kansas City. Both offers were attractive financially as well as intellectually.

One evening the phone rang while Florence and Leon were having dinner at their home on the Purdue campus with dear friends from their hometown. It was the Senior Vice President from the Kansas City Fed.

He said, "Leon, the President of the Bank and I have decided to increase our offer to $12,000."

That was more than several of the professors at Purdue were making at the time. The conservative nature in Leon won out. He would accept the position if the Bank would allow him to take an international consultancy for up to three months if one were offered.

They agreed. Leon placed a blurb in the *American Journal of Economics* that he was available for up to three months.

The three years in Kansas City were pleasant and rewarding for both Florence and Leon. They enjoyed their new split-level house. George and Gwen were in excellent schools and could walk to the near-by community swimming pool during the summer.

Leon bought a small electric organ and patiently taught Gwen to read music and play it. After two years, her IQ scores at school had increased 10 points to a large extent, they were told, because of the stimulation to the brain from reading music and playing simple pieces on the organ.

Florence taught school while earning a master's degree, with emphasis on teaching reading, at the University of Missouri in Kansas City. Leon enjoyed a plush office at the Bank, a pleasant and efficient secretary and gourmet lunches in the Executive Dining Room. He wrote about the farm economy in the Tenth Federal Reserve District and gave talks before bank and farm groups. On a busy day his phone would ring twice.

Then he had a call from John Auer in Washington, D.C., who said he was recruiting officer for the Agency for International Development, U.S. Department of State. He had noted in the *Journal* that Leon would be available for up to three months. They were seeking an agricultural economist for a two-year assignment in Pakistan.

"Would you be interested?"

In the ensuing discussion Leon learned that Chuck Elkinton, who was Agricultural Attaché in Tokyo when he and Lowell Hardin were there in 1960, was in charge of USAID/Pakistan's agriculture program. Leon was interested.

*The Hesser Family in Kansas City, 1965*

He told superiors at the Kansas City Fed that he would be resigning to take a two-year assignment in Pakistan. A couple days later Dr. Ray Doll, Leon's direct supervisor, said the President of the Bank had authorized a two-year leave of absence if he would consent to take it. Leon said he would have to decline because he did not want to be committed to returning to the Bank; he might want to stay in the Foreign Service.

Ray said, "You do not need to make a commitment. We will give you a two-year leave and if you decide you would like to return to the Bank, you may." How could one refuse that!

In early January 1966 Leon flew to Washington, DC for six weeks of orientation at State Department. Dear Florence stayed behind to supervise the packing of household effects, which would be placed in storage until their return. She drove from Kansas City to Washington with the two kids in a new stick-shift Mustang; they had been advised that automatic shifts were not a good idea in the Asian Subcontinent.

In the ensuing three decades and some twenty moves to different houses in nearly as many countries, Florence was inevitably left behind to supervise the packing of household effects. She concluded that one of the fundamental principles that Foreign Service people learn in State Department orientations is that the wife must be in charge of household moves.

## Chapter Seven

## Pakistan Revisited

The Hessers had a delightful home leave during the summer of 1968, following their first two-year tour in Pakistan. During their second tour, they were assigned to Islamabad, the country's brand-new capital in the foothills of the Himalaya Mountains. The move of the USAID Mission from Karachi to Lahore in 1966 had been an interim move until sufficient housing became available in Islamabad to accommodate the staff.

Islamabad had many advantages. Near the top of anyone's list was the weather, which was far superior to that of humid Karachi and was even better than the dry heat of Lahore. General Ayub Khan, the beloved President of Pakistan, had selected a site near his boyhood home for the new capital.

About 15 miles northwest of Islamabad are the ruins of the ancient city of Taxila, which was founded in about the sixth century B.C. Situated at the meeting-place of three great trade routes, Taxila flourished for more than a thousand years; it was at its zenith when Alexander the Great descended on the Punjab in the spring of 326 B.C. He spent a few weeks at the important city and left a garrison there before proceeding further east.

Though Alexander's troops remained for less than a decade, archeologists have found traces of the Greek influence in the shape of coins, pottery and other small objects. The site was an interesting diversion for curious expatriates, especially the women, who often had time on their hands – Florence was among them.

The Hessers were placed in what seemed to them a mansion: a huge living room, five bedrooms and six baths. A large house was needed because they would be doing a lot of official entertaining. By the time they moved there, Florence had learned well how to manage a cadre of servants. They were fortunate to have acquired Karim, who was from the Chittagong Hill Tracts in East Pakistan and had previously served as chef for families from several different countries. His range of dishes was huge. Leon could call Karim at 10 a.m., tell him he was bringing six official guests for lunch and he would have a banquet ready. He was amazing not only as a cook, but as captain and quarterback for the other servants, which included two full-time bearers, a lawn-maintenance man and a night guard, plus a part-time derzi (seamstress) and dozi (clothes-washer). As efficient as they were, Florence said many times she would trade the whole cadre for an automatic washing machine and a dishwasher!

Among the projects under Leon's supervision were two to help develop Pakistan's two agricultural universities. The Agency had arranged a contract with Washington State University to provide a team of professors and administrators to help develop the West Pakistan Agricultural University at Fazilabad and a similar contract with Texas A & M to assist the East Pakistan Agricultural University at Mymensingh. The mutually agreed objective was to evolve these institutions on the pattern of the U.S. Land Grant universities, incorporating the three-pronged functions: teaching, extension and research. In India at this same time, the U.S. was helping develop 12 land-grant-type agricultural universities. In both countries, the pattern was to have U.S. professors substitute for local counterparts while the latter were in the U.S. to get advanced degrees and learn about the land-grant system. Americans can be proud of the result.

Another project for West Pakistan was called Precision Land Leveling – for the huge irrigated Punjab, "the land of the five rivers."

The rivers flow from the Himalaya Mountains and converge at the southern part of the Punjab into the huge Indus River, which flows to the Indian Ocean. The Punjab is one of the largest irrigated areas in the world and was potentially one of the most productive.

A problem noted early in his tour by Curry Brookshier, Leon's deputy who grew up in an irrigated area in Texas, was that the land being irrigated was invariably not totally level.

After a heavy irrigation, he saw wet spots intermingled with dry spots in virtually every field. When he and his expatriate extension staff pointed this out to farmers, they would always say it was as level as they could make it; it would have to suffice.

But Curry was not satisfied. He had his Agricultural Engineer, Nile Dimick, work with a local machine shop to fabricate a land-leveling device to be operated on the rear of a Massy Ferguson farm tractor, of which there was at least one in every neighborhood.

The markedly increased yields obtained from demonstrations of this precision land leveling machine, used in combination with a surveyor's tripod, soon convinced alert farmers that their land was not really level after all. The project assisted a number of local manufacturers to fabricate the machine and within a few years the devices were in operation throughout the Punjab with remarkable results.

Progress in impoverished East Pakistan, where rice rather than wheat was the main staple, was going much more slowly. New rice seed varieties from the International Rice Research Institute (IRRI) in the Philippines were introduced and were making some improvement in rice production, but substantially less than the potential. Leon formed a team to do an analysis and the team designed two new projects specifically for East Pakistan. One was a large rice production project with 12 expatriate advisors; it would be based on a more widespread introduction of IRRI varieties plus improved husbandry. The other project was to help build a strong research program at East Pakistan Agricultural University aimed at alleviating constraints in food production.

In late 1969 it was time for Leon to fill out another COAR. This time he truly wanted to stay in the Foreign Service. He selected the Philippines and Indonesia as his first and second choices for a new assignment when this one ended in the summer of 1970.

A new Mission Director, Joe Wheeler, had recently arrived to replace Bill Kontos. Joe called Leon to his office when he saw his COAR.

He said, "Leon, if you leave I will have no continuity in the agricultural program because both of your deputies (one for East and one for West Pakistan) are scheduled to leave. I would really be grateful if you would return for a third tour."

Leon said, "Joe, what I *really* would like would be a year of educational leave."

They talked for a while longer. Finally, Joe said, "How about a semester at Harvard as a Visiting Scholar and then return with us for a third tour."

With no hesitation, Leon agreed. Florence would be delighted. Gwen, who recently had joined her American School classmates as they took their senior class trip through the Khyber Pass to Kabul, Afghanistan, was now at Mount Ida Junior College in Boston, and George was at Middlesex prep school, just a few miles from Boston.

Before they left for home leave a senior program officer from Washington came out to review planned activities, especially the plans for new projects in East Pakistan where the Agency was interested in helping redress the balance between East and West. He said, "Are those two proposed projects for East Pakistan really good ones?"

Leon said, "They sure are; for two cents I would return to Dacca myself to oversee their implementation."

The next thing he knew he had two cents in his hand! Joe Wheeler agreed that Leon and family could reside in East Pakistan; with frequent travel and the newly installed, quite remarkable communication device, Telex, Leon would remain responsible for USAID's agricultural programs in both East and West Pakistan.

The fall semester at Harvard in 1970 was a delight for Leon. He audited a variety of courses oriented to the international sphere and wrote several papers. The time was refreshing and relaxing for Florence as well.

Leon was asked frequently while on campus whether East and West Pakistan – one on the east side of India and one on the west – would remain as one country.

His answer was always, "No. It may hold together for six months or maybe for six years, but sooner or later the country will split – the bond is just not strong enough."

Leon and Florence arrived in Dacca, East Pakistan to begin a third tour at 11:50 pm on February 28, 1971. At noon the next day Shaikh Majibur Raman made the impassioned speech that led to massive demonstrations. Tensions between East and West grew for the next few weeks.

On the night of March 25, the Hessers attended a party at the home of Archie Blood, the U.S. Counsel General for East Pakistan. Guests included a half-dozen American couples besides several from other countries. The Bloods were gracious hosts; they showed the Bogart-Hepburn-Bacall movie, *The African Queen*, followed by a sumptuous dinner. Shortly after 11 p.m. guests from other countries began to go home.

About midnight the Americans started to their respective homes only to find that the rebels had put roadblocks at all the main streets. They returned to the Bloods' home where from midnight until 4 a.m., from the flat roof of the residence, they watched the fires, bombs and tracer bullets all over the city.

Leon went to bed at 4 a.m. About 8 o'clock Florence woke him to announce that senior officials from West Pakistan had taken – kidnapped – Shaikh Majib from his home just a couple blocks from the Bloods' residence and flown him to West Pakistan. Leon said, "The sons of bitches." Nearly all Americans in East Pakistan were sympathetic to the East, the underdog.

Within a few days the American Ambassador in Islamabad ordered all but the most essential official Americans evacuated from Dacca to places like Bangkok, Ankara or the United States. He did not want any of them to come to Islamabad for fear they would say or do something embarrassing to the U.S. government. Joe Wheeler told the Ambassador he would really like to have Hesser return to Islamabad and said, "He will not talk."

The Ambassador agreed. Joe wasn't so sure that Florence wouldn't talk, so he arranged for the wife of his deputy to take Florence on a two-week sightseeing trip to Afghanistan. She could talk all she wanted to over there.

Between April and November 1971 Leon flew back and forth between Islamabad and Dacca, a couple weeks on each side. Because of India's strong sympathy with East Pakistan in the conflict, PIA could not fly over India; they had to go down around the tip of the country. Leon's main duty on those trips was to analyze the food situation in East Pakistan and report the results to Washington. He did a statistical analysis – technically called multiple linear regression – using the best data he and his Bengali colleagues could muster.

Relevant variables included acreages of various varieties and types of rice, use of fertilizer and irrigation, and the acute political situation that resulted in an almost total collapse of the agricultural credit system as well as large-scale migration of farm laborers.

The Mission cabled the 20-page report, *Rice Production in East Pakistan:*

*Prospects for the Year 1971-1972,* to Washington together with a strong recommendation that large-scale imports of food grains were essential to avert mass starvation. Washington responded with shiploads of food aid. In his files Leon has a letter on White House stationary from Maurice Williams, who headed a White House Task Force for East Pakistan, thanking him for the "Hesser report" which formed the basis for the U.S. government's plan for food aid.

Leon was in his Dacca office in November when the Indian Army began to cross the border into East Pakistan to oust the West Pakistan Army. The Indian Army had an obvious logistical advantage. The day before Thanksgiving, Leon was lying in the sun at his Dacca residence when the Provincial USAID Director drove up and said, "Hesser, I want you on the next plane out of here; The Indian Army is on the march."

Leon said, "You don't have to tell me twice." He flew back to Islamabad where he finished out the tour with what a Washington colleague called "a full Mission, half a country and no program." East Pakistan was now Bangladesh. As Leon had predicted, Bangladesh would now receive more international assistance and develop better than it would have as a stepsister to West Pakistan.

It was COAR-time again. Once again Leon indicated a preference for either the Philippines or Indonesia for his next assignment. Shortly, he had a call from Don McDonald, Assistant Administrator of USAID in the State Department building in Washington.

He said, "Leon, I would like for you to come to Washington as my senior agriculturist in the Asia Bureau."

Leon said, "Sir, I was thinking I would like to go either to the Philippines or Indonesia."

McDonald said in a rather commanding voice, "Leon, I would like for you to come to Washington!"

"Yes, sir."

## Appendix to Chapter Seven


## Exploring the Desert in Pakistan
*by Florence E. Hesser*


O ne of Leon's assignments while we lived in Pakistan was to evaluate sites in the desert where "water-harvesting" dams might be placed to an advantage. A consulting engineer had recommended to Leon that a series of earthen structures laid out in fishbone fashion in selected areas of the desert could enhance substantially the usable water from the infrequent rainfall. Bill Kontos and Leon decided to evaluate the sites together. Joan Kontos and I went along. Living in Pakistan was generally boring for expatriate women, so we were happy to take the two- or three-day trip.

I had become close friends with Joan, a quiet, intelligent and happy person. Her father had worked for many years in Albania, so she had been exposed to overseas assignments before she and Bill took up an international career with the State Department.

We departed on the exploratory trip in the desert on a pleasant day in the winter of 1968. We were to stay the first night at a rest house along the way where dinner would be awaiting us. We arrived in a jeep with an experienced driver.

Upon arrival we were joined by members of the local government. One of the men proudly displayed a small new car to which Joan and I were assigned the next morning. The fellas followed in the jeep. The men knew where they were going but Joan and I would have never found our way back if we had been left along the road unescorted.

Pakistani men, such as the government officials who had joined us, had seldom if ever experienced women accompanying their husbands on such a trip. Their wives were left at home with the children, covered with burkas when they left the house. American women were indeed a novelty. The owner of the car drove, since the car was his. It became questionable whether he had had any lessons in driving prior to purchasing his first car. However, this thought did not cross our minds as we climbed into the back seat.

It was creeping up on noon by the time we left the Rest House and headed across the desert. The Pakistani men had on business suits. Joan asked if they would like to put their suit-coats on the back seat. They both turned almost all the way around at this suggestion and were paying more attention to us women in the back seat than to the driving.

We were barely moving when Joan took their coats; they turned to look straight ahead again. By now, the driver was losing control of the car and we were on the shoulder of the desert road. Luckily the hill at the side of the road was not steep but, as the driver attempted to straighten the car, he became nervous and lost control. Before we knew what was happening, the car rolled slowly over and over, down the hill into a field. Leon and Bill, who were watching, said it looked like a keystone silent movie.

But Leon was frightened. He jumped from the jeep and ran to the car. I had landed on top of Joan and was on my back looking up through a window, which was now on the top of the car. Leon was looking down through the window at me. The look on his face was one that I shall never forget.

He was so frightened, but he said the real problem was that my skirt was over my head! The contents of our purses were scattered. The driver was also frightened – the car, of course was damaged and we had to leave it in the field for someone else to rescue. The driver held the key to the ignition in his right hand, which was injured; he had literally twisted the key out of the ignition and broke it off trying to shut off the engine. We were all fine, laughing hysterically at the way we looked and the mess we were in. We all climbed into the jeep and returned to the rest house, which was fairly close to the scene of our accident.

We took account of our injuries, which luckily were few, washed up and enjoyed a fun supper as we all felt well acquainted by the end of the day's ordeal. We laughed about being "dam specialists" and "out standing in our field." We were sorry that the new car had been damaged, but the owner seemed less concerned than we. The trip continued the next day without mishap.

## Chapter Eight

## Florence Matriculates at Ball State

In August 1972, six months before Leon was to be reassigned to Washington, the Hessers prepared to put Gwen and George on a plane to Boston where they were both in school: Gwen at Mount Ida Junior College and George at Middlesex prep school. Gwen had been admitted to Mount Ida as a special two-year, non-degree student majoring in art.

Before going to Mount Ida she had shown substantial progress in painting under the tutelage of Kohari, one of Pakistan's young and upcoming artists. The experience at Mount Ida was to broaden and deepen her interest in art and help her grow socially and become more independent.

As the Hesser family moved from place to place, George had bounced from public schools in West Lafayette, Indiana and Overland Park, Kansas to American Schools in Karachi, Lahore and Islamabad.

In the process he was switched from traditional math to "modern math" and back to traditional math to the point that he had a block on mathematics.

One of the teachers at Lahore American School had said to Florence: "You must accept the fact that George is not college material." (George was eventually to earn a BS degree in Engineering while remaining on the "Dean's List," but that is another story.)

Part of George's problem was that the new American School in the brand-new city of Islamabad, where George had taken his high-school freshman year, was not yet as strong as it needed to be. Another was that George's study habits in that environment were a bit sub-par.

In this situation his parents offered George two options: he could go to the Murree Hills School in northern Pakistan, run by missionaries, or to a prep school in the States if he were to be admitted. George preferred the latter.

Applications were sent to five of the top prep schools in the eastern United States. Four of them sent pink slips. David Sheldon, Headmaster at Middlesex, thought he could see a pearl in the oyster; he was intrigued by George's varied experiences, especially his having lived in Pakistan, and despite his less than stellar grades agreed to accept him – even serve as his advisor – if George were willing to repeat the 9th grade. George agreed. During the first three years at Middlesex, George had shown brilliant growth. It was now time for him to return to Boston to begin his senior year.

As Florence was helping Gwen and George pack for their journey to the States, she said once again to Leon, "I wish there were someplace here in Pakistan where I could do some more graduate work."

There wasn't.

Leon said, "Why don't you get on the plane with the kids, go back to Indiana and visit a couple of schools, say Ball State University and Indiana University, to see if they might admit you at this late date to do graduate work leading to a doctor's degree."

Florence liked the idea. She spent the next few days getting ready. Then, she accompanied Gwen and George to Boston and proceeded on to Indiana. She visited both Ball State and IU.

Especially in the Education Department at Ball State, professors and administrators welcomed her with enthusiasm. Within a few days she was admitted as a candidate for an Ed.D., a doctorate in education, and embarked on a fast track to complete the required coursework within one year. After registering, she rented a nice apartment within walking distance of the campus.

It would mean a long six months apart for Florence and Leon, between August and February, but they broke up the time in two ways. Leon flew back to Indiana for a 10-day vacation during the fall, to help furnish the apartment, see the campus and meet the Ball State Teachers College faculty under whom Florence was to study.

Florence flew to Islamabad for a month over the Christmas holidays to complete her research at the Gujranwala Literacy Center where she had worked as a literacy advisor for USAID. With the blessing of the Center's staff, she made copies of some 10 years of data the Center had collected, detailing results of their literacy program under different assumptions. These data would be the main basis for her dissertation.

After Christmas, Gwen joined her mother in Muncie, Indiana where she attended beauty school and took driver's training.

At Ball State, Florence's interest in international literacy reform struck some of the faculty as a bit far out, but they encouraged her to gather the information and use the subject for her dissertation.

She was thrilled with Teacher's College and selected J. David Cooper as her major professor after meeting him three times in interviews. She was impressed with the appearance of Dr. Cooper's office at Teacher's College.

It reminded her of Leon's offices, neat, orderly and organized. In addition, Dr. Cooper was always on time and ended his meetings promptly as scheduled. He was friendly, informed, considerate and interested in the international aspects of Florence's study.

Another graduate student had told Florence to be sure to take all the courses that Dr. Cooper offered as they were the best. However, she should *never* name him as her major professor because he was too meticulous and demanding.

Based on this and, again, on the positive comparison with Leon and his approach to work, she decided that Dr. Cooper was the person she would select. This proved to be a wise choice as Dr. Cooper supported Florence every day with her work, read the chapters of her dissertation promptly and offered guidance at each step of preparing the dissertation.

As Florence read, researched and wrote about the Literacy Center in Guyranwala, her interest in international programming and in the subject of literacy grew. Her doctoral committee insisted that her study include more than a mere description of a literacy center abroad so she researched other international literacy programs.

She interviewed Dr. Bhola at Indiana University and Dr. Robert Laubach, son of the famous Frank Laubach of "Each One Teach One" fame, in Syracuse, New York, and incorporated some of their theories and experience in her dissertation.

By taking an overload, Florence was able to complete all the required courses at Ball State in twelve months. After completing the course work she joined Leon in Washington where she worked half-time for one year at The George Washington University while she finished her dissertation.

*Florence receives the doctorate of education
degree at Ball State University, 1975*

Leon helped her purchase a condominium at Ocean City, Maryland where she was able to retreat on weekends and during vacations to write and study alone. She had always loved the ocean and swears that a sea captain must have been in her ancestral background. Why else would a gal from the Midwest who had not seen the ocean until she was almost 40 love it so?

Florence says, "Leon's understanding and help during those years made the relatively short time to accomplish the doctorate both financially possible and without stress."

They had both observed that many couples split during the years they work on a doctoral project, largely because of the pressure while the student pursues his or her goal alone. However, Florence had cooperated fully with Leon while he did his work at Purdue; the experience proved valuable and Leon was a big help to Florence as she completed her dissertation.

Two years after Florence finished her doctorate, the dissertation, *Village Literacy Programming in Pakistan,* was published by the University of British Columbia. This reflected highly on her Ball State University doctoral committee. Florence had told her advisor when she entered graduate school, "I have my dissertation theme picked and much of the research gathered. What I need is a committee to help make this work professional and worth publishing. The degree, to me, is just icing on the cake."

## Chapter Nine

## Exciting Times in Washington

Washington is a fabulous place. After a few months, the Hessers wondered why they had resisted being assigned there. The professional jobs of both Leon and Florence were exciting. They had an apartment in Columbia Plaza, just a 10-minute walk to either of their offices, or to the many evening performances at the new Kennedy Center, or to any number of wonderful restaurants. What more could they ask?

Leon had a nice office in the Department of State building on C Street. He was head of the agricultural assistance program for the Asia Bureau of the U.S. Agency for International Development. In that capacity he made trips of varying lengths to Indonesia, Bangladesh, and South Korea to help the USAID Missions in those countries do agricultural sector assessments or outline strategies to enhance food production. The seven years of experience in Pakistan proved to be invaluable in his new assignment.

During Leon's first six months in Washington, from February to August 1973, Florence was still in residence at Ball State University in Indiana. Every few weeks, one or the other found time to join the other for a rendezvous, which added romance to their lives and helped relieve the ache of their being apart.

During that spring, Leon was pleased to be joined by son George whose last semester in his senior year at Middlesex consisted of serving in Washington as an Intern to Indiana's Senator Birch Bayh.

What an exciting and charming introduction to the nation's capitol! Then, in late summer, about the time Florence joined Leon full-time in Washington, George along with Mark Norris, his roommate for four years at Middlesex, ventured off to Colorado College in Colorado Springs.

On one of Florence's visits to Washington from Ball State, she and Leon chatted about what she might do after she finished her degree.

Leon said, "Why don't you go introduce yourself to the Dean of Education at The George Washington University," which was practically across the street from their apartment, "and see what interest he may have in your background."

The Dean got real excited. It turns out that the woman who had headed the Reading Center at the university had just told the Dean, one time too often, that she was going to resign, if . . . . This time, he had accepted her resignation. After the Dean and Florence had visited for awhile, he said, "How would you like to direct our Reading Center?"

That was like a dream come true. Florence said she would really like to do that, especially if she could serve half-time for the first year while she was completing her dissertation. They shook hands on the deal.

By its very nature, the Foreign Service means times away from home. And while Leon had not been given the chance earlier to serve on a longer-term assignment in Indonesia, he was asked to go to Jakarta for six weeks to help them form a development strategy.

In preparation, he read a lot of background papers and books on Indonesia, some of which were by Professors Wally Falcon and Carl Gotsch of the Food Research Institute, Stanford University. Leon had become well acquainted with Wally and Carl when they had been to Pakistan to do some analyses for him. They were first-class scholars and great to work with. So, on the way to Jakarta, Leon stopped at Stanford and picked their brains.

A major issue for Indonesia was what to do about overcrowded Java and the larger but under-populated outer islands. Jakarta's USAID Mission had sought help to analyze the issue – how should they advise the Government of Indonesia and provide some resources to help stimulate adjustments. Leon made trips to a few of the outer islands in his initial on-the-ground research.

A substantial difference existed in the natural resource bases, both among the outer islands and between Java and the outer islands. For the long-term development of the country, it would make sense to capitalize on these differences; each island should produce under the principle of "comparative advantage" according to its resources, and let market forces move the commodities and services among the islands to the benefit of the entire population.

Easier said than done. A more efficient transportation system would be needed, for one thing, to move commodities in trade among the islands, and services in the outer islands needed to be enhanced in order to attract workers away from Java. The Mission accepted Leon's report and, with concurrence from Washington, held discussions with Indonesian government officials. Together, they began to implement the recommendations.

Several years after his trip to Indonesia, Leon met a colleague from the Indonesia USAID Mission who said, "The Hesser report is still one of the pillars of our development policy."

Bangladesh was another challenge. Leon was asked to put together a team to analyze the country's agricultural research system and make recommendations for restructuring it. On this assignment, he had the good fortune of having three top-notch individuals as members of the team: Dr. Guy Baird, whose background is discussed in more detail in Chapter Eleven; Dr. Floyd Williams, who had been the agricultural research specialist on Leon's staff in Pakistan, and Dr. James Miller, a specialist in campus architecture from Kansas State University.

Less than two years earlier, the new country of Bangladesh had been East Pakistan. The bulk of Pakistan's agricultural research resources were employed on the West side. Neither East Pakistan nor the new Bangladesh was tied very well into the international agricultural research system.

The Ministry of Agriculture had elaborate plans for a new agricultural research facility at Joydepur, a few miles outside Dhaka, to replace existing facilities that had become surrounded by the sprawling capital city. Professor Miller cringed when he saw the plans – buildings would be spread out over much of the acreage available for both buildings and research plots, leaving little space for field research. Fortunately, only a small amount of construction had already begun.

Dr. Miller drew a rough sketch of an alternate configuration for buildings and outlined a plan for more extensive research plots, which was the facility's main reason for existence. The Bengalis liked the new plan. So did officials of the World Bank, who agreed in principle to finance construction. Professor Miller then drew the plan in more detail.

Guy Baird and Floyd Williams articulated the potential advantages to Bangladesh of taking a more aggressive approach to being tied into the growing set of international agricultural research centers and reorganizing their efforts more toward "adaptive research" and trials on farmers' fields rather than doing "basic research." For the more sophisticated, basic work, they could draw on the international centers.

Five or six years later, Leon was in Dacca on another assignment. He was escorted to Joydepur by the Director General of the Bangladesh Agricultural Research Council who gleamed with pride. The new facility was being supported with both USAID technical assistance and World Bank financing for bricks and mortar. He had reason to be proud: positive results were already evident in increases in quantity and quality of food available to their rapidly growing population.

Meanwhile, Gwen had married a young man from the Hesser's hometown in Winchester, Indiana. A few years later, they presented the Hessers with their first granddaughter, Sharon.

George studied Liberal Arts for two years at Colorado College. When Gwen vacated her bedroom in the Washington apartment, George decided to come live with his parents and study engineering. Since his mother was on the faculty, he could attend The George Washington University tuition-free.

In defiance of the teacher at the Lahore American School who had told his mother that her son was not college material, George consistently was on the Dean's list. The combination of prep school, liberal arts at Colorado College and engineering at GWU helped George to be one of those rare engineers who can write well! He joined Dupont after graduation.

He met, courted and later married a beautiful, talented and charming colleague, Kimberly Ott, also a Dupont engineer. They have three beautiful, talented and charming daughters.

## Chapter Ten

## Florence Joins The
## George Washington University Faculty

I n the fall of 1973, Florence became Director of the Reading Center in
the School of Education at The George Washington University. Over
the next 20 years, in spite of lethargy from some elements of the
university's administration, she developed the Center into one with international acclaim.

At the time she became Director, the Reading Center had a small program and only five faculty and staff members, so Florence was able to manage it easily during the first year on a half-time basis while she finished her
dissertation. Once her dissertation was finished, and she had a year's experience behind her, she began to add programs to enrich the value of the Center's
chief function – helping graduate students learn improved techniques to teach
reading in schools.

The centerpiece of her philosophy was to bring in real people – individu-
ally or in groups – for the graduate students as well as her faculty to work
with, to learn by doing.

As part of their learning process, at no cost to the families, graduate
students were assigned under supervision of qualified staff to test individual
children with reading problems and then tutor them for several months to
get practical experience. The graduate students helped the children become
familiar with public libraries and encouraged them to read.

Reading Center staff and graduate students also worked with groups of children of similar age from the Washington area, in after-school or Saturday classes. One popular course was titled Math-on-the-Mall. The children were exposed to concepts of mathematics by learning about the form and dimensions of the Washington and Lincoln monuments and the expanse in between – the Mall.

In the process, they also delved into related historical and social issues. A similar type of course was called Life at the Zoo; the children studied about the animals that they observed being fed and cared for. The graduate students as well as the children were learning by doing.

*Professor Hesser organizing a production*
*to be performed before the students' parents*

People who were encouraged to participate in the Center's programs ranged from gifted youngsters to children with reading problems to adults who wanted to improve their reading skills, or even *learn* to read. Both the graduate students and those from outside who participated in the various programs appreciated the new emphasis.

One of the adults who wanted to learn to read was a 40-something, well-dressed, handsome and obviously successful black businessman. He owned a commercial cleaning company that spanned four states and had the potential of expanding. He came to Florence's office, closed the door and said, "Could you teach me to read?"

His face was visibly distraught. As he explained his ego-deflating circumstance, he shed tears. His wife, whom he had encouraged and helped to get a university degree, did all the paperwork – reading, writing and correspondence – while he handled the workforce and daily demands of his business.

Except with his wife, he had covered his inability to read and write and often carried a newspaper under his arm to imply that he could read. He desperately wanted to be able to read and write.

Florence explained the Reading Center's policies and programs, which included tutoring adults either on a one-to-one basis or in small groups. He chose one-to-one. Florence assigned Hilda Warner, a jewel of a person and a great teacher of adults, to work with him. Within six months, the new student was reading well at an adult level. The deep appreciation he showed motivated Florence and Hilda to expand the sweep of their adult literacy programs.

Over the span of her career, many people had said to Florence, "You know, there are those who just will never learn to read and who are not college material."

Yet, in the 20 years that Florence and Hilda worked together in adult literacy programs, including with many handicapped persons, they encountered only one – a seriously handicapped teenager – who was unable to learn to read. With patience and encouragement, they concluded that almost anyone could be taught to read.

Outside the U.S. Government, The George Washington University was one of the largest employers in the District of Columbia; this included service and maintenance personnel in each of the university's many departments.

Among the potential advantages of working for the university were tuition benefits. A common problem among the service personnel was their inability to pass the university's entrance exams because they could not read well enough.

Florence and her staff let it be known that they could help those who truly wanted to become degree seekers. Over the years, the Reading Center staff helped scores of the university's service employees earn degrees by raising their reading abilities through tutoring. The displays of gratitude to Reading Center staff from these employee-students were often emotional.

A new dimension that Florence brought to the Reading Center, especially with some of the more challenging cases, was actively to involve other elements of the university in diagnosis and prescription: the Speech and Hearing Department, the Psychology Department, and even doctors in the School of Medicine. She expanded the hours that the Center was open, to include evenings and Saturdays, and encouraged active parent participation.

As one of her non-university undertakings, Florence took the lead in establishing an adult literacy program in the District of Columbia under the umbrella of the national organization, Literacy Volunteers of America (LVA).

Sarah Goodwin, who had had relevant experience in the New York City Christian Center, assisted her in this effort; after her retirement from the Christian Center, Sara worked for 10 years with Florence in The George Washington University Reading Center.

Florence subsequently served for many years as a member of the board of the national Literacy Volunteers of America organization whose headquarters are in Syracuse, New York.

Whenever an opportunity arose, Florence encouraged international exposure for Reading Center staff and graduate students. She and five of her staff attended, at their own expense, an international conference on educational technology in Prague in August 1991.

It turned out to have been an even more exciting adventure than they had expected. On the second day of the conference, news broke of the attempted coup in Moscow in which Yeltsin had stood on the tank and defied the Communist government.

Among the delegates in Prague was a contingent of about 30 educators from the Soviet Union, headed by a Vice-Minister of Education. They were terribly frightened. They all had families back home. If this were the beginning of a revolution, should they return to their families or stay in Prague? Some of them wept uncontrollably. They were unable, psychologically, to participate further in the conference. They walked the halls and talked about what they should do.

Because Florence and her staff could not understand the local radio and TV reports, she asked her staff in Washington to fax her relevant news items from the *Washington Post*. Carol, the Reading Center's secretary, stayed up all night cutting and pasting articles on fax paper and sending them to Prague via the fax machines on display by vendors at the conference.

From the literally yards of material sent, it was apparent that people in the United States, as well, were excited about this development in Moscow. After digesting the articles, Florence and her staff retired to bed.

Next morning, when she went to the makeshift newsroom, Florence found that Carol's long sheets of materials had been cut up into individual articles. She was puzzled until she learned that the Soviet delegation had faxed them to teachers, relatives and friends all over Russia and other republics of the Soviet Union.

Florence was not to realize the full significance of this until six weeks later, when she learned that teachers in Moscow who had received the faxes from their colleagues in Prague had distributed copies of the news to the soldiers who were in the vicinity of the tank on which Yeltsin had stood.

Meanwhile, when they learned that the military action had ended within three or four days, that Yeltsin had made his point, the Soviet members of the conference went ballistic; they danced until the wee hours of morning and vodka flowed freely.

Six weeks later, during the second week of September, Florence was in Sochi, on the Black Sea in Southern Russia, at the invitation of the Soviet Minister of Education, undoubtedly due to the congenial meetings in Prague. Leon went along to carry Florence's briefcase.

The purpose of the Conference was two-fold: to bring together all prominent Russian educators and make them known in the international community of educators, and to expose them to ideas and experience largely unknown in Russian educational circles.

Florence participated in the discussion group on teacher training which was led by Dr. Yulia Turchaninova, whose official position at the time was Chair of the Pedagogy and Psychology Department in the Russian Federation's recently established Educators' In-Service Training Institute.

To put the Sochi conference in context, Yulia says, "From April 1985, when Gorbachev came to power, through the summer of 1991 life in the USSR did not change much; the economy was still going down, the KGB and the Communist Party were still controlling everything, but some important changes in spiritual and mental domains were slowly occurring."

Among the major fields of change were in foreign affairs, media and education. Yulia said, "The country was becoming more open and the will to integrate into the international community was very strong.

"The launch of intensive communication and cooperation between Russian educators and their foreign colleagues was in my opinion one of the most important results of the conference." The conference stimulated the beginning of a long-term friendship between Florence and Yulia.

Yulia explained later that she had been one of those who had distributed the materials that had been faxed from Prague, and had – on the spot – cheered and actively supported Yeltsin as he stood on the tank in defiance in August 1991; four months later the USSR collapsed and Yeltsin became President of the Russian Republic.

## Chapter Eleven

## Leon Becomes Director, Office of Agriculture

As perhaps his most challenging assignment, after one year in the Asia Bureau, Leon was asked to head the Agency's Office of Agriculture and coordinate U.S. agricultural assistance programs world-wide.

He managed an office of five divisions, with a $50 million per year research and technical assistance budget aimed at enhancing food production in less developed countries of the world. This included coordination of the United States contribution to the growing family of international agricultural research centers of the type that sparked the Green Revolution in South Asia.

Dr. Omar Kelly, who had been Director of the Office of Agriculture for a number of years, had decided to retire and go back to his home state of Colorado. As one of the three most senior agricultural officers in the agency, Leon was tapped to replace him. Omar Kelly was a tough act to follow, and there would be only a one-month overlap before Omar departed, but Leon agreed to accept the challenge – partly because his good friend Guy Baird, who was Associate Director of the Office, would be a solid pillar of support.

Dr. Baird had come to the Agency from a career in agricultural research with the Rockefeller Foundation. He was intimately familiar with the rather new but rapidly growing set of international agricultural research centers that had sprung from earlier work, supported heavily by the Ford Foundation and the Rockefeller Foundation, which led to the creation of the International Center for Improvement of Corn and Wheat (CIMMYT) in Mexico and the International Rice Research Institute (IRRI) in the Philippines. The Green Revolution, made possible by the high-yielding varieties of wheat and rice from those two centers, alerted the world to the benefits of this kind of highly focused research.

Omar Kelly and Guy Baird had done much of the staff work that led to the creation of the Consultative Group for International Agricultural Research (CGIAR). The CGIAR is co-sponsored by the World Bank, the United Nations Food and Agriculture Organization (FAO), the International Fund for Agricultural Development (IFAD) and the United Nations Development Program. It has offices in the World Bank complex in Washington and is charged with coordinating financial contributions from various sources, primarily from European countries, Japan, the United States and several foundations, but including smaller amounts from a number of other countries.

The United States had challenged all other donors and potential supporters of the CGIAR system by pledging to pay 25 percent of the total cost of maintaining the set of international centers if the others would cover the remaining 75 percent.

When Leon was still in the Asia Bureau, Omar Kelly had chaired a meeting that included Leon and his counterparts in the other three regional bureaus. Kelly sought the group's implicit support of the 25 percent pledge for CGIAR. Leon expressed strong support, based to a large extent on his having witnessed first-hand the unprecedented results in South Asia.

The other three regional agricultural officers hedged a bit, likely stimulated by a bureaucratic fear that such a pledge might eat into their portion of available funds. In any case, the Administrator signed off on the 25 percent pledge.

As Leon's Associate Director for Research, Dr. Baird accepted the demanding responsibility of serving as liaison with the CGIAR staff and monitoring progress of the individual centers in the system. The world responded to the challenge of increasing support to the centers and new ones began to be added under the umbrella of the CGIAR. CIMMYT and IRRI were the initial shining stars, but the family began to include other stellar centers. During Leon and Guy's tenure in the Office of Agriculture, in addition to CIMMYT and IRRI, the set included:

- CIAT: The Centro Internacional de Agricultura Tropical. Colombia. Mandate: Increase the region's production of common beans, cassava, rice, and beef.

- CIP: The Centro Internacional de la Papa. Peru. Mandate: Develop technology for increased production of the white, or Irish, potato.

- IBPGR: International Board for Plant Genetic Resources. Headquartered in FAO, Rome. Mandate: Promote an international network of genetic resource centers to further collect, conserve, and document plant germplasm and make it available to scientists for research.

- IFPRI: International Food Policy Research Institute. Washington, D.C. Mandate: Identification and assessment of issues arising from the intervention of governments and international agencies in national, regional and global food production.

- IITA: International Institute of Tropical Agriculture. Nigeria. Mandate: Worldwide responsibility for the improvement of cowpea, yam, cocoyam and sweet potatoes.

- ICRISAT: International Crop Research Institute for the Semi-Arid Tropics. India. Mandate: Improve the quantity and reliability of food production in the semi-arid tropics.

- ILRAD: International Laboratory for Research on Animal Diseases. Kenya. Mandate: Assist in the development of effective controls for two major livestock diseases: trypanosomiasis and theileriosis.

- ILCA: International Livestock Center for Africa. Ethiopia. Mandate: Assist national efforts in tropical Africa by carrying out research and development on improved livestock production and marketing systems.

Leon says, "History will most certainly show that the set of international agricultural research centers stand out as one of the most significant global institutional developments of the twentieth century."

The five divisions in the Office of Agriculture during Leon's tenure were:

- Economics Division, headed by Dr. Lehman Fletcher, on loan from Iowa State University;

- Crops Division, headed by Dr. Earl Leng of the University of Illinois;

- Livestock Division, headed by Dr. Ned Raun, on loan from the Rockefeller Foundation;

- Soil & Water Division, headed initially by Dr. Donald Plucknett and later by Dr. Dean Peterson, formerly Vice President, Utah State University; and

- Fisheries Division, headed by Dr. Douglas Jones, a career USAID Foreign Service Officer.

The staffs in these divisions were tasked with responding to the needs of USAID missions world-wide. This sometimes meant their going to the countries themselves on short-term assignments for analyses and consultation. More often, it meant recruiting top-level specialists from U.S. universities or research institutes to carry out the assignment.

Congress had authorized USAID to make grants to select universities and research institutes to, in effect, internationalize their domestic strengths and provide short-term technical assistance as needed overseas. For example, Auburn University, which was preeminent in the United States in the science and application of aquiculture – the controlled production of fish in ponds – was given a grant to extend the technology to poorer countries that requested it through USAID. This proved to be a very effective way to provide the best possible technical assistance to less-developed countries.

Another mechanism that proved effective was the Collaborative Research Support Program (CRSP). Dr. Earl Leng, Chief of the Crops Division, was primary author of the CRSP concept: eminent scientists in one or more U.S. universities work on common problems in concert with a number of key scientists in developing countries to solve problems to the benefit of both the United States and the less-developed countries. A prime example was work to enhance the protein content of cereal grains, such as wheat, corn and grain sorghum.

The end result of all these programs was an effective and efficient system of enhancing the quality and quantity of food for poorer people in developing nations. Americans can be proud.

John J. Gilligan, former Governor of Ohio, had been appointed Administrator of USAID in 1977. He was proud of his Agency's accomplishments, but after being on the job for about a year he had come to some conclusions. In reflecting on the situation, he very likely had in mind a statement that was attributed to the British at a time during World War II when thousands of American troops were stationed in England, to wit: "The trouble with American soldiers is they are over-paid, over-sexed and over here."

In a reflective moment in a meeting in which he assumed there were no reporters present, Mr. Gilligan said, "The trouble with my Agency is there are too many people who are over-graded, over-paid, over age, and over here."

By too many "over here," he meant there were too many people in Washington shuffling papers and too few serving overseas where the action was. To Mr. Gilligan's embarrassment, his statement was widely reported in newspapers.

At about that time, the Personnel Office of USAID was breathing down Leon's neck. They were doing their job. Leon was a Foreign Service Officer rather than a Civil Service Officer, which meant he was expected to spend the bulk of his time posted overseas. He had been in Washington for five years, which was stretching the limit without being reassigned. Personnel advised him that the position of Chief, Agriculture Division, USAID Mission to Chad was open. "Would you be interested?"

Leon was one of only three Foreign Service Officers whose specialty was agriculture who had achieved the rank of FSR-1 (GS-18 equivalent), the highest rank in the Foreign Service for non-political appointees.

Partly because a move to Chad, a rather non-descript country in central Africa, would have been a step down, but more importantly because he did not want to pull Florence away from her career at The George Washington University, he was inclined to take early retirement.

Foreign Service Officers had the option to take early retirement if they were over 50 and had at least 20 years of U.S. Government service, at least five of which had been overseas. Leon was 53 and had more than enough service time.

Another reason he considered retiring was a temporary change in the retirement eligibility rules that was being discussed in Congress as an incentive to reduce the number of government employees. Rather than basing one's retirement annuity on an average of the "high three" annual salaries, Congress was proposing for those who would opt to retire during a three-week window in October 1978 that the annuity would be based on one's highest annual salary, dubbed "high one."

Considering all factors, Leon decided to "jump out the high-one window." At his retirement party, he recited this poem:

*I've Had My Fill*

*I've had my fill of continuing resolutions*
*And optimal solutions and starting Revolutions;*
*Admitted, they were not always Green;*
*And so with mixed emotions*
*I shall no longer ply the oceans,*
*But embark upon a life that's more serene.*

*Don't get me wrong!*
*My career has been rewarding,*
*The Agency's served me well,*
*And I might have stayed in longer*
*Were it not for Personnel.*
*Sometimes I felt like telling them to . . go . . to . . . . .*
*Chad. I wish I had!*

*It was not an easy decision,*
*But when all was said and done*
*I chose that ultimate option: High One*

*So now, dear friends, please be of good cheer,*
*The Administrator need no longer fear*
*That I am over-graded, over-paid,*
*Over-sexed, and over here.*


Leon retired on Friday, October 6, 1978 and went to work on Monday, October 9 as a consultant.

## Appendix to Chapter Eleven

## A City Girl's View of New Agricultural Technology
### by Florence E. Hesser

Leon has enjoyed working at virtually all levels of agriculture (except hoeing the vegetable garden). He has always been especially interested in new agricultural technology that promises to bring some extra income to the world's farmers. Of particular interest in the mid-1970s was the novel idea of the disease-free, farrow-to-finish hog operation.

When we were young tenant farmers in the 1940s and 1950s, he built several of a new kind of individual hog house with electric heat lamps to shelter and comfort the mother sow and babies when she had her pigs. (My remembrance is that pigs usually arrive in February when the weather in Indiana is terrible.)

With this type house he could easily feed the sow and count the pigs while doing some quick math in his head – this many pigs, weighing 200 pounds each at market time in the fall, at $25 per hundredweight – to estimate his income for the season.

My mother, who was city wise and farm wary, had warned me that life as a farmer's wife had a dark side: farm animals are unclean and they smell bad, especially when it is wet and rainy and you have to walk from the house to the barn.

"You will have to wear knee-high boots," she said knowingly. "The manure will be knee-deep." She had told me this when I had just taken my second shower for the day and was doing my hair and makeup for a dinner date with my future farmer-husband.

We had left the farm in 1955 and it was now Easter 1975. Leon was excited. He had learned that between Washington, D.C. where we were living at the time and his parents' farm in Randolph County, Indiana, was a beautiful new farm operation near Dayton, Ohio that housed 100 sows and all their little pigs in one building. It was a long, long, one-story building with exhaust fans placed in round holes at regular intervals to bring fresh air into the building.

With a big smile, he told me as we started the 10-hour drive to his parents, after my hair had just been fixed for Easter Sunday and my Easter clothing was hung carefully in the car, that we would have enough time to stop and I could see this new hog technology. Being a quiet person, of German ancestry, he did not wait for a response but moved quickly to pay for his gasoline and check the car.

We arrived at the appointed place in Ohio and rang the bell – one cannot just walk into a high-tech hog operation. The owner-operator, who was expecting us, answered the door and welcomed us midst the sound of oinking pigs. He explained that to enter a disease-controlled environment like his, one must take a shower, wash one's hair and put on a sterilized suit and shoes as well as a plastic cover for the head.

I informed Leon that I could not go in as my hair-do, acquired at Watergate Beauty Salon at the price of a day's wages, would not withstand a shampoo in a hog barn.

"And remember, tomorrow is Easter Sunday."

Leon mumbled for a few minutes to the owner and explained that his wife really needed to see this; I suspect he said that she had not been close enough to a pig in 20 years that she could possibly be a swine-disease carrier.

They improvised. I could put the shoe covers over my shoes and the "overalls" over my slacks and sweater; then they had a plastic garbage bag that I could use to cover my hair-do. I looked very much like someone from outer space as I entered the confines of the sows, piglets and the smell of hog manure. I thought *Mother was so right!*

The owner, two farm hands and Leon were very busy talking, walking up and down the long building, counting piglets, admiring sows and discussing dollar signs; the number of pigs one could raise per sow – and per worker – was far more than was possible in the tiny buildings Leon had used when he farmed. Meanwhile, I stood to the side and entertained myself by watching the baby pigs.

I have always enjoyed watching baby pigs. They are basically very clean animals – one of the few animals that consistently use a corner of their pen for a bathroom – and the piglets each have their own faucet which they return to for meals on a regular basis. These faucets are available only to a sow's own piglets. Momma can tell her own by the way they smell. I say this is a real art in a pigpen where the corner is used for a bathroom!

Seemingly, the piglets are assigned faucets according to their strength to defend the location – the strongest gets one up front while the weakest piglet gets the very last faucet – "the hind tit" – deep between mother's hind legs. It was entertaining to watch the piglets fend for their position in line with their siblings and seemingly talk to each other.

I believe they would say something like, "Go get your own tit; this one is mine!"

All the time the mother sow talks to her pigs in a low soothing voice, feeding 10 to 12 babies all at one time.

Unfortunately, as I walked slowly down the concrete walkway, outside the gates that housed the pigs, I stopped in front of one of the round windows that housed one of the big exhaust fans. At that moment the fan came on (it was activated by a timer, I found out later); it literally ate the plastic garbage bag covering my expensive hair-do.

The noise – both the sucking sound and my yelling – attracted the men in the room, who came running to my rescue. That ended our visit; I was quickly escorted out and helped out of the jump suit and shoe covers. They helped pat my hair back in place and gave me a Coke to calm my nerves. (I could have used something stronger!) I returned to the car, mentally eating humble pie. Mother was *so* right!

## Chapter Twelve

## Washington during the Carter Administration

F lorence says, "The capstone of my professional career was 20 years as Professor of Education and Director of the Reading Center at The George Washington University in Washington, DC."

Among the many exciting experiences was an after-school program for gifted children in which Amy Carter participated for four years.

The whole world leaned forward to get a view of this new family as they unexpectedly got out of their limousine, after President Carter was sworn into office, and walked up Pennsylvania Avenue with their skipping and bouncy nine-year-old daughter, Amy, between them. When President and Mrs. Carter moved into the White House in January 1977, they were just five blocks from the GWU Reading Center.

One morning at breakfast, Florence tested an idea with Leon: "I am thinking of informing the Carters about our summer program for children."

"Great Idea," Leon agreed.

Florence's letter to the First Lady was short and to the point, indicating that five blocks from the White House was a program that Amy might enjoy attending during the summer. The University would do everything it could to protect her security and privacy. She could be brought to the building by the back garage entrance and come to the fourth floor by a quiet and secure elevator. Her welfare would be a major focus of the Reading Center staff. She would have the opportunity to make a group of friends her own age during the six weeks of classes.

For the spring semester, the Carters had enrolled Amy in Stevens Elementary School a short distance from the White House. President Carter was dedicated to supporting the public school system. Having been a student at public schools himself and as a parent having served on the school board in Plains, his dedication was real and serious. Amy was the first President's child in the 20th century to attend public school while the father was President. She adjusted well and breezed through the spring semester at Stevens Elementary School.

The Reading Center staff was electrified when a few days before the summer program was to start a small envelope arrived from the White House with a completed form to enroll Amy and a check for the tuition signed by Rosalynn Carter.

An attached note asked Florence to call Carol Benefield, Mrs. Carter's secretary, to make arrangements. Florence says, "Nervously, I rang the number; I found Ms. Benefield to be bright, congenial and cooperative." Florence explained that they were having parents' orientation in the Reading Center library on the first day of class.

Florence met with Dean Tillman to tell him of the new student. He was elated.

Hilda Warner, a dear and dedicated instructor in the Center, exclaimed later, "The Reading Center was a small, insignificant backwater until 1977 when it suddenly became part of the main stream of the university."

Ms. Benefield called Florence to confirm that Mrs. Carter would personally bring Amy to the first class and participate in the parents' orientation. She said the press would be invited as it would be better than excluding them and get criticism for doing so.

Parents of the eleven children enrolled in the class for nine-year-olds were to gather at 11 a.m. The Reading Center staff put the place in order and fixed cookies. Florence carried her punch bowl across the street from the apartment to serve refreshments for the mothers. They anxiously awaited arrival of the First Lady and "The First Kid."

Members of the Secret Service arrived first. They placed cords along the hallway to restrain visitors and guide the press. The number of press persons was overwhelming; they filled the hall.

In the middle of the turmoil, a small man in a dark suit carrying an average size brief case strolled into the Center. Quietly, the Secret Service surrounded him. With one on each side, they literally lifted and carried him to the elevator and out of the building. The startled man did not have a clue what was going on. He was an innocent telephone repairman whom Florence had called the day before to solve a minor telephone problem.

Fifteen minutes later, the gracious First Lady arrived with her daughter. Amy was escorted to her class and Mrs. Carter retired to the small library. The other mothers came on schedule, not suspecting that Mrs. Carter was there.

As each one entered she arose, introduced herself and shook hands. With grace, she put each startled mother at ease. The meeting went forward as if nothing unusual was afoot. The First Lady ate cookies and drank punch with the other mothers and chatted about her child.

Florence says, "We were all fascinated by how commonplace and gracious she was. She impressed everyone that she was truly interested not only in her own child but everyone else's as well. The First Lady was indeed a lady first!"

That was the beginning of a fascinating four-year relationship. Amy attended every session during that first summer and proved to be an intelligent, well-adjusted and happy child. She made friends. She completed homework. The main thing that set her apart was the attention she attracted. She disliked having her picture taken. If by chance someone showed with a camera she would slip under a table and hide.

Near the end of the summer session Florence indicated to Mrs. Carter that the Center staff was of the opinion that Amy had special talents and was most likely a gifted child. They proposed to spend some time testing her, as they were doing with some of the other children, so they would know the level of her intelligence and more about how to channel her instruction, educational experiences and extracurricular activities.

Florence says, "It has always been important to me to include parents as much as possible in children's school activities."

A day in which the University was not in session was selected for Amy's testing. Special testing rooms were used in which Mrs. Carter could observe the testing without Amy's knowing she was being observed. Florence explained each step of the test to Mrs. Carter as Dr. Eva Johnson, Reading Center Psychologist, administered the tests. While Dr. Johnson was grading the tests, Florence and Mrs. Carter exchanged small talk and laughed about their daily goings on.

In an hour or so, the tests were graded. Florence and Dr. Johnson went over the findings with Mrs. Carter. The results showed that Amy was indeed a gifted child. At one point Mrs. Carter interrupted to say, "I wish Jeemie could hear this! Would you consider coming to the White House to tell him what you have told me today?"

Florence says, "Of course, I agreed!"

A phone call from Carol Benefield confirmed that the Carters would see Florence the following Wednesday at noon, at one of the regular Wednesday noon sessions the Carters reserved for private talks. The hour in the Oval Office with President and Mrs. Carter passed quickly. President Carter initiated the discussion by saying, "We're here to talk about my favorite person, Amy."

*Florence's first parent conference with*
*President and Mrs. Carter, in the Oval Office*

Florence says, "A lasting memory is of President Carter's penetrating blue eyes conveying that I was being studied and evaluated as we talked. Both President and Mrs. Carter were warm and friendly."

Pictures were taken that Florence continues to treasure. Then, Florence told them of the plan she had put together for an After School Program that could accommodate Amy and other gifted children in the fall. The Carters graciously endorsed the plan. The program continued for twelve years, enriching the lives of hundreds of gifted children in the Greater Washington area.

*Florence welcomes President Carter to an end-of-semester
production of Kabuki for parents of children in the after-school program*

Subsequent to the meeting in the Oval Office, the Carters attended parents' meetings and the children's programs at the end of each semester. On one occasion, they went to the Japanese Embassy where the children made a presentation based on that semester's studies of Kabuki. Ambassador and Mrs. Togo greeted the children in a reception line that required each child to follow a protocol in which each shook hands as if they were young adults.

Tiny hamburgers and hot dogs as well as Japanese food were served in the gorgeous dining room with its enormous, historical chandelier. Members of the Japanese Embassy assisted each child, described the food and helped them serve themselves and be seated. What a remarkable learning experience! Following tours of the Embassy, the Japanese children and the after-school children performed for the adults.

One day Mr. Dobrynin, the Ambassador from the Soviet Union, called the White House to enquire if it might be possible for Amy to play with his eight-year-old granddaughter. Amy, then eleven, felt she was now too old to "play" with anyone. Hoping not to disappoint the Ambassador and his wife, Mrs. Carter called Florence to ask what might be done to cover this awkward situation.

Florence suggested that they might repeat for the parents assigned to the

Soviet Embassy a performance that the children in the after-school program had recently given for their parents. Mrs. Carter liked the idea. Florence arranged with Sidwell Friends Lower School to use their auditorium. They would serve food on the covered patio after the entertainment. The school was walled, so security would not be a problem. A Russian lady was assigned to coordinate their children's part of the program and a choral group was engaged.

The evening was a great success. The children – both Soviet and American – performed beautifully and had lots of fun doing it. The performance ended with the Soviet children teaching the American children the Virginia Reel, which they had not been exposed to before. They all laughed hysterically as the American children stumbled through the movements.

Both the Soviet and the American parents brought food. Families became acquainted. Children, including Amy, exchanged names and phone numbers; Ambassador Dobrynin's granddaughter was in the middle of it all. Having obviously enjoyed the evening the Soviet parents stayed on to visit.

They were friendly, warm and gracious. It seemed ironic that the Cold War was in full swing at that time. Florence says, "Our children learned more that evening than we could teach them in weeks through reading and pictures."

Florence continued, "A lasting memory is when the lovely Russian lady who worked with us to arrange the program called late one night to tell me goodbye. She and her husband were returning to Moscow. She told me how she had enjoyed our friendship and she added, 'I luff you!'"

One semester the children studied Shakespeare and at the end of the term they put on a performance, *Excerpts from Shakespeare*. Mrs. Carter attended, but the President had to miss. A few days later, Florence had a call from Mrs. Carter asking if the children might do a repeat performance in the East Room of the White House. Florence readily agreed.

The Carters invited members of Congress, the Cabinet and the Supreme Court

*First Lady Rosalynn Carter and daughter Amy invited Florence's two aunts (middle) and a cousin to visit in the White House*

who had children this age or a special interest in children. Leon confessed later that tears rolled down his cheeks because of the exquisite performance of the children. It was truly a novel evening.

There was only one mishap: banners that had been hastily hung fell on the volunteer adult Renaissance Orchestra, causing one of the little boys' hats to fall off and reveal that it had been down-sized with toilet tissue.

Following the production, refreshments were served in the State dining room. Parents, children and teachers all felt honored to participate in the First Family's evening entertainment series at the White House.

Before the presentation, Florence called to ask Carol Benefield if she should prepare an introduction for the program. Carol had replied that she did not think it would be necessary, as the President would normally greet everyone and introduce the children and the performance would begin.

Upon arrival at the White House that evening, Florence met Mrs. Carter on the stairs leading to the East Room. The First Lady said, "Florence, here is what we will do. I will introduce you and you can introduce the program."

As she seated herself beside Leon, across the aisle from the Carters, Florence whispered to him, nervously, "I am going to have to introduce the program!"

As Mrs. Carter began to introduce her, Leon turned to Florence and whispered, "STAND UP!"

Florence says, "To this day, I feel weak as I think of that moment! All I remember saying was, 'Please realize that we are not going to take this show on the road.' Laughter followed, causing me to relax so I could explain the After School Program and the evening proceeded as planned."

## Chapter Thirteen

## Leon's Career as a Private Consultant

ollowing his retirement from USAID, Leon enjoyed another 22 years of interesting and productive work as a consultant, in and out of Washington, helping 20 countries of Asia, Africa, Eastern Europe, Russia and Ukraine develop sustaining increases in food production for the masses. The efforts were financed through the World Bank, the Food and Agriculture Organization of the United Nations, the International Fund for Agricultural Development, or USAID.

An early consulting assignment was for the World Bank in the quaint little country of Malawi in east central Africa. Leon headed a team of three to analyze the country's agricultural research and extension system and make recommendations to improve its performance.

A quickly identified problem, common in many small countries, was that the best-trained, top-level scientists were spending the majority of their time on administrative details. Anyone with an administrative problem went to the scientist-administrative head of the research organization, or of its sub-units, to seek a solution.

To outsiders, the remedy seemed simple – establish a strong administration unit to handle issues that do not require scientific analysis, and free up the scientists to do what they were trained to do. That sometimes required adjusting salary levels so that research scientists could be paid as much, or more, than the administrative heads of units.

*Leon and Florence were exclusive guests for a
traditional dance in rural Malawi in East Africa*

Other suggested adjustments included establishing a national council to review problems that need the attention of the research establishment and set priorities to focus scientific efforts; getting the country's research system tied into the international agricultural research centers; and – importantly – strengthening the interaction between the research system and the extension agents who are responsible for conveying improved technology to farmers. The World Bank accepted the plan and provided multi-year financing to implement it.

Within a few weeks, the World Bank asked Leon to head a 10-person team to do a similar analysis in Zambia, next door to Malawi. Zambia is a much larger country and in many ways more complex. Because overland roads were not extensive or well developed, the team chartered a plane to get to the several outlying research stations.

Most of the main issues were similar to those of Malawi, as were the proposed solutions. Whereas Malawi at the time had Kamuzu Banda as "President for Life" and a rather stable government, the political situation in Zambia was more fickle.

The Bank negotiated a loan on soft terms to implement the plan, and some work was started, but much of the implementation was delayed due to disagreements within the country.

As Leon crossed the Atlantic on return from Zambia, he met a colleague on the plane who told him, "RONCO Consulting Corporation has just been awarded a two-year contract to develop the agriculture of the Caribbean country, St. Vincent and the Grenadines. They are looking for a good team leader."

When Leon got off the plane in Washington, he called Steve Edelmann, RONCO's Executive Vice President, and said, "I hear you have a job for me in St. Vincent."

Steve, who had been following Leon's career, was elated. He said, "I'm going down this week-end to negotiate the contract – I'll stop by tomorrow and get your resume." That was the beginning of a fruitful 15-year relationship between RONCO and Leon.

The two years in St. Vincent, with a population of less than 100,000, was an absolute delight. Besides being a nice place to live, it was an interesting project: organizing farmers to grow fresh vegetables to ship to the States during the winter. A North Carolina farmer was engaged to help with production technology of zucchini, cucumbers, yellow squash, watermelon, and bell peppers.

A former Dole employee was hired to establish a centralized cooling system to remove field heat from the vegetables and organize timely shipment in roll-on, roll-off refrigerated containers. "Watermillion" was new to the residents – it was a big hit in the local markets.

Florence took a year's sabbatical from the university so that she, Gwen and Gwen's six-year-old daughter Sharon could join Leon during the middle 12 months of the assignment. Sharon still talks about the experience as the best year of her life. She quickly became acquainted with many of the friendly residents of the island. The family was far out in the Caribbean on a four-day vacation cruise when another sailboat passed by. Passengers on the other boat waved and shouted, "Hi Sharon!"

A three-month assignment in Albania was an interesting, though in some ways bleak, contrast to that of St. Vincent. Until the iron curtain fell, Albania had been the most closed-off to the outside world of any of the East Bloc countries. The country had been ruled with an iron fist from 1944 to 1985 by dictator Enver Hoxha.

Some 3,000 large concrete bunkers scattered throughout the country, mostly along the coastline, were a stark reminder of the harsh leadership. The bunkers were to be manned by rural militia who had been trained to fend off the Americans who, the people had been told, were expected to invade. Virtual anarchy followed the downfall of Communism and the people welcomed Americans with open arms.

The mission was to outline a plan to reorganize agricultural research and extension to accommodate the needs of thousands of small-scale, private farmers as opposed to the old system that was designed to serve only a handful of very large state farms.

There were no suitable hotels so Leon's six-person team stayed in two houses in Tirana, the capital. Leon was the cook for the three people in his house. They had a rule: the first person to complain about the food becomes the new cook. At each meal, no matter how bland the food, the guys would say, "Hey, Hesser, this is great stuff!"

The team involved the Albanians in discussions of concepts as the research and extension plan progressed. In the end the plan was well received.

At times, Leon was the trouble-shooter for RONCO. As one example, on a Wednesday afternoon Steve Edelmann came to Leon and said, "I would like you to leave this Friday to go to Dakar, Senegal; we have a problem that needs urgent attention." It was a USAID-financed watershed management project, involving four West African countries, that was coordinated by a multi-country agency in Dakar.

Two problems existed with the project that was nearing an end: (a) RONCO's team leader, who was highly proficient technically, was not adept at writing the final report in English, his second language, and (b) the USAID Mission had some differences with the coordinating agency, the counterpart group that RONCO's technical assistance team had worked with.

Leon handled the first problem, writing the final report, with relative ease, but he was caught in the middle of the political battle. As USAID and the coordinating agency negotiated their positions, Leon had to re-write the report a couple of times.

The last night before the report was to be presented formally to USAID, Leon stayed up all night to make the adjustments in the report required by the negotiated positions. As USAID's project officer, an engineer, came to the meeting to discuss the report, even before he sat down he said, "Hesser, you used the wrong tense in the foreword."

This was more than the normally calm and cool Leon could take. He slammed his fist on the table and said, "Goddammit, we stayed up all night re-writing the report to accommodate your negotiated changes, and you criticize our choice of tense in the foreword!"

There was dead silence for awhile. "Then," Leon says, "we had a good meeting."

He had taken a lesson from his good friend, Professor John Mellor of Cornell, who once told him, "Leon, the secret to blowing your top is knowing the right time to do it."

Leon was once asked to join a team in Jordan sponsored by the International Fund for Agricultural Development. He confesses that the substance of the team's one-month mission was not that exciting, but some related instances were. One evening as he was having dinner in the Intercontinental Hotel in Amman he struck up a conversation with the British woman who had served for several years as nanny to King Hussain's children.

In addition to living with the Royal Family in the palace, she frequently had traveled with the King and Queen and their children. She said in his private life King Hussain was one of the most kind and considerate persons she had ever met. The first-hand account was indeed heartening.

Two exciting events occurred on a weekend trip from Amman to the southern tip of the country to examine port facilities at Al Aqaba, on the Gulf of Aqaba which flows into the Red Sea and is Jordan's only outlet to the sea.

En route, the team stopped for a few hours to view the vestiges of the magnificent ancient city of Petra, Jordan's premier tourist site. Nestled in the mountains, Petra was hand-carved by the Nabataeans from nature's multicolored stone several centuries before the birth of Christ. The city, located at the crossroads of ancient trade routes, flourished for centuries as a trade center and afforded protection against rogue invaders. Petra is one of the marvels of the ancient world.

Shortly after they departed Petra, the driver stopped so the team could interview a local farmer. The stop seemed impromptu at the time, but in retrospect it was undoubtedly a staged event.

An open-sided tent was erected to shade the visitors. After chatting a few moments, the farmer absented himself while he went to slaughter a lamb. About two hours later, servants brought to the tent a huge mound of rice

piled on what looked to be the well-polished top cut from a 55-gallon oil drum.

The lamb's roasted parts were strung about on top of the rice. At the very top of the mound was the lamb's head. The food, which was eaten with fingers of the right hand, was marvelously delicious. Leon made out pretty well until a servant poured gourmet gravy over the mound, after which the sauce ran down his arm and dripped off his elbow.

As is the local custom with guests, the farmer-host graciously pulled choice pieces of meat from the heap and hand-fed each of the three members of the team. The team leader and Leon were thusly fed one each of the creature's eyes, the quintessence of the feast and an honor to the guests.

Leon was involved in several short-term activities in a number of other countries: Kenya, Poland, Hungary, Bosnia, Russia, Grenada, Jamaica. He made more trips to Egypt on assignment than to any other country. He says a most satisfying activity there was one initiated in 1995 to help private farmers produce and export fresh fruits and vegetables to Europe.

Though Egypt has obvious natural advantages in climate and location, the potential had not been exploited for a number of reasons. The task of RONCO's project team was to mitigate or eliminate the constraints. Leon served as home-office coordinator of the project and made a number of on-site visits.

Among the constraints were varieties that suited Egyptian tastes but differed substantially from Europe's preferences. RONCO introduced appropriate varieties for export together with the technology required to meet Europe's demanding standards.

To maintain a reasonable shelf life of the fruits and vegetables, it was essential to introduce and maintain a "cold chain." This required pre-cool facilities to be established at or very near farmers' fields to remove quickly the field heat from the harvested items, trucks with refrigerated containers to move the produce to the port or airport, and proper holding facilities at the port while planes or ships were awaited.

Early in the project, most of the produce had to be sent to European destinations by plane, which was costly, because proper ships for transporting fresh produce were not yet accustomed to dropping anchor at Egypt's ports.

With RONCO's help in developing markets for the produce in key European markets, together with the development of the cold chain within country, by the end of the seven-year project the volume of the commodities shipped had grown to the point that shipping lines were competing to transport the produce. Everyone agreed that the project had been a great success.

Not all assignments to Egypt turned out so rosy. In 1979, Leon headed a 10-person team to carry out a USAID-funded study of the technical and economic feasibility of land reclamation in the desert. The relevant concept of land reclamation was putting down wells to tap underground seepage of Nile River water that was transported in irrigation canals. The Government of Egypt was looking for an analysis that would support their desire for donor funds on soft terms to finance large-scale reclamation.

The basic conclusion of the six-month study was that under existing policies (too much governmental control), land reclamation as they defined it was not economically feasible – the Egyptian economy would be better off investing in projects other than land reclamation. The report did have a set of recommendations that, if followed reasonably, might enhance the economic prospects. USAID was pleased with the study; Egyptians remained silent for awhile.

A few months later, Leon was asked to head a team to outline a 20-year perspective agricultural development plan for the Sinai Peninsula. The Government had already invested substantial resources to run a series of six huge siphons to transport Nile water under the Suez Canal to be distributed as irrigation water in Sinai.

Several days after the team had arrived, Leon was advised one day that he had a meeting at 7 p.m. that night in the office of the Minister of Development, whose ministry had responsibility for land reclamation. Only the Minister was there.

It turns out that the Minister had just returned from Washington where he had hoped to secure a commitment of funds for reclamation. In a meeting at USAID, the Assistant Administrator showed the Minister "the Hesser report" and said, "But, Mr. Minister, this suggests that land reclamation is not a very good investment for your country."

Upon his return to Cairo, the Minister learned that the person who was head of the team for the Sinai study was that same @%#&* Hesser. For about 20 minutes, the Minister lambasted Leon up one side and down the other. When he finally stopped to catch his breath, Leon said in a calm voice, "Mr. Minister, may I respond?" The Minister kindly consented. In a few sentences, Leon sought to assure the Minister that he would be completely unbiased in carrying out the Sinai study.

After the meeting, Leon went directly to the home of the American representative of the company that had the prime contract for the work in Egypt. After explaining the nature of the conversation with the Minister, Leon said, "Either he got it off his chest and we will never hear about it again, or he will want me on the next plane out of here. I want you to know that if it's the latter, I'm prepared to leave."

The representative said, "I'm not! I want you here!"

Nothing further was ever heard of the issue. By using their imagination, the team was able to put forth a number of useful approaches to developing farming systems in micro areas throughout Sinai, but it would never be the country's breadbasket.

## Chapter Fourteen

## Florence in Saudi Arabia

B y its being in the nation's capital, The George Washington University Reading Center was often patronized by people from other countries: graduate students studying improved techniques of teaching reading, or children being enrolled in the Center's after-school program for gifted children, or children being tested and tutored to diagnose and improve their reading skills. As an example, one British family came to the Center three times from London to have their daughter tested and to consult on techniques to help the child read and comprehend.

One day Florence was presented a challenge by a representative of Saudi Arabia's Royal Family. The representative said that two of a Saudi family's children had been tested and tutored by Reading Center staff and the family had been impressed with the marked improvement the tutoring had made in the children's ability to read and comprehend. The representative said, "Dr. Hesser, would you consider replicating this Reading Center in Saudi Arabia?"

What a challenge! They briefly discussed alternative models for such a venture. Then Florence said, "Let me think more about it and I will get back to you in a few days."

The Saudi representative said, "Think about it, and propose a budget. We will fund it."

That evening, as she relayed to Leon her conversation, Florence was both elated and quite overwhelmed at the prospect of working with the Saudi Royal Family on a project that, if carried out successfully, would have significant and positive long-term implications for the Kingdom.

The following brief on the Royal Family may help one to understand Florence's apprehension. During the first third of the twentieth century, Abdul Aziz united the fractious tribes of the Arabian Peninsula into a unified country. He had married daughters of several tribal leaders as one means of uniting the tribes. It had been common in Arabia for men to have more than one wife.

The Kingdom of Saudi Arabia was founded in 1932 and Abdul Aziz was proclaimed King.

Prince Faisal bin Abdul Aziz was the second of the many sons of Abdul Aziz, and was a favorite. He was groomed by his father for big things. In 1919 the British government had invited Abdul Aziz for a goodwill visit to London. For various reasons he was unable to go; instead, he sent his 14-year old son Faisal, who became the first member of the House of Saud ever to visit Western Europe.

During the five-month trip he met with many officials and had an audience with King George V. He saw his first typewriter, telephone and airplane and was fascinated by escalators in the stores. This mission initiated Faisal's career as the twentieth century's longest serving Foreign Minister.

In 1932, Foreign Minister Faisal had an extensive tour of Europe and Russia. Near the end of the tour he sailed on the steamer *Pravda* from Baku to the Persian shore of the Caspian Sea. At Constantinople he met Iffat al Thunayan, a beautiful red-headed girl of Saudi ancestry whom he recognized immediately as having remarkable personal qualities, and he took her back to Jeddah to be his wife.

By some accounts Prince Faisal had led a wild youth, but Iffat changed that. Faisal settled down with Iffat to a marriage remarkable in its time for the comparative equality between the partners. Their children, including the girls, were educated privately by English nannies at home, then sent abroad for further studies. Compared with most children of the Saudi Royal family, the children of Faisal and Iffat were unspoilt.

Iffat was intelligent, articulate and forceful; she was to bring about major changes in the new Kingdom. In the 1930s there were no schools for girls in the Arabian Peninsula. While she strove to broaden Saudi education as a whole, starting schools for girls was a special concern of Iffat. She provided the land and funds in 1956 for a home for "orphaned" girls; they would be taught to read.

The first year only 15 little girls attended, but slowly the idea of teaching girls to read and write began to catch on. Twenty years later, about half as many Saudi girls as boys were in school. In the 1960s Iffat funded and opened a teacher training school in Riyadh to train female Saudi staff to teach in the new girls' schools.

This concern for education is the heritage passed on by Prince Faisal and Princess Iffat. It was their children, especially the daughters and daughters-in-law, who were now proposing to sponsor the new Saudi Reading Center.

In 1964, Faisal was designated *King* Faisal ibn Abdul Aziz. When Faisal was proclaimed King, Iffat became known popularly as "queen," though that title did not officially exist in the Kingdom.

King Faisal's 11-year reign was marked by humility, honesty, thrift and attention to detail. Faisal's father had united the Kingdom; King Faisal made substantial progress toward making it a modern state before he was assassinated in 1975.

Florence discussed the Saudi proposition with Leon, who had spent his career in international economic development and was often involved in strengthening human-resource institutions. The two concluded that the best way to assure that a center would serve the needs in the new environment would be to select a group of Saudis to come to The George Washington University to do Master's degrees plus practicum work in the Reading Center.

These mature graduate students, both men and women, could then return to Saudi Arabia and make the adjustments necessary to start a center in their own culture.

The sponsors arranged for Florence and three key members of her staff to fly First Class on Saudi Airlines to Riyadh to discuss the concept with members of the Royal Family. They were met at the Riyadh Airport by the family's driver and Neuha, the eldest daughter of Princess Lulua, who gave each of the four visitors an abaya, a silk navy-blue robe with a silk scarf for the head and face. They were to wear these whenever they were outside their hotel rooms, unless they were inside a home or room where only women were present.

At their hotel, they met initially with Dr. Bakalla, a college professor who served as Florence's chaperone each time she came to the country. Florence learned later that Dr. Bakalla had come to Washington where he had quietly surveyed the Reading Center and, apparently, had given a positive report to the Royal Family before they asked Florence to consider replicating the Center in Saudi Arabia.

During the week in Saudi Arabia, in addition to Professor Bakalla, Florence and her team had meetings with Queen Iffat's daughters, Princesses Sara, Latifa and Lulua, and with sisters-in-law, wives of the princesses' brothers. The purpose of the meetings was for Florence to explain the philosophy of her Reading Center at GWU and exchange ideas on ways to approach the task of replicating the Center in Saudi Arabia.

As one basis for their making decisions, to get an indication of how parents would respond to a center where they could bring their children for testing and evaluation, Florence conducted an informal needs assessment at three different meetings with parents. The response was overwhelmingly positive; a high percentage of the parents who attended had children who experienced difficulty reading and comprehending.

Among the several sessions during the trip was a sumptuous dinner around a large round table at the exquisite palace of Princess Lulua; the gathering included all the sisters and sisters-in-law. Princess Sara, the eldest of the sisters, speaking on behalf of all of them, expressed appreciation to their visitors and gave approval in principle to launch the project.

*Florence and two colleagues prepare to interview graduate-school candidates in Saudi Arabia*

Back in Washington, Florence wrote a draft proposal, outlining the objectives, structure and rationale for the project and the suggested approach to accomplish the goals. Representatives of Saudi Arabia and the university signed off on the concept and the budget.

Before Florence and her team's second trip to Riyadh, about six months after the first, the Saudis advertised widely, outlining the required qualifications and indicating that a team from GWU would interview candidates to go abroad for study and then return to implement the new Saudi Reading Center.

On the second trip Florence's escort, Dr. Bakalla, arranged a conference room at the hotel for candidates to be interviewed. Florence and her staff interviewed 64 men and women from whom they selected 20 – ten men and ten women.

Florence says, "A precious memory of the second trip to Saudi Arabia was our bouncing along through the desert with Princess Lulua in a luxurious van upholstered with red velour. We were off to see a project sponsored by a brother of the princesses; he was experimenting with irrigation using desalinized water to grow vegetables."

The Prince admitted that this was an expensive way to produce vegetables, but it might help move the country toward food security by reducing dependence on imports.

The group enjoyed a delightful picnic in the desert. The main purpose of the trip, it turned out, was for the Prince and his lovely wife to get to know Florence; Lulua and her sisters wanted the Prince's support for the reading center project.

A few weeks after the second trip, the 20 Saudi candidates arrived in Washington and embarked on their training program. Each was to strive toward a Master's degree and also work in and study the procedures of the GWU Reading Center.

In 1990, during her third visit to Saudi Arabia to report on the project's progress, Princess Lulua arranged an evening meeting for Florence and her team to visit with Queen Iffat in the lovely, historic palace in Jeddah. This was an honor, indeed.

Dr. Bakalla escorted the four women to the palace. As was the custom on these trips, each member of the team wore the abaya until she was well inside the palace doors. A servant met them, took the abayas and folded them before placing them carefully on a shelf.

Since they would be only in the company of women they would not need them until time to leave the palace. Princess Lulua – tall, thin and gracious – walked across the parlor to greet Florence and her team. Then, she took them across the room to meet Queen Iffat, who remained seated. Queen Iffat welcomed them and asked Florence to sit beside her on the couch so they could visit.

The room was beautifully appointed with fresh flowers and a plentiful supply of Arabic sweets in lovely dishes. Stately palm trees were visible through the windows onto the garden. Servants offered dates – fresh, plump and delicious – and served Arabic coffee in tiny white cups with gold edges. The Queen and Florence both sipped the coffee for about 15 minutes, the normal custom prior to any serious discussion.

Florence presented Queen Iffat with a gift – a small ceramic tea set that daughter Gwen had hand painted especially for her. Queen Iffat accepted the set graciously. The Queen's eyes sparkled as Florence explained progress of the project. Throughout the session, Queen Iffat was as gracious and friendly as she was beautiful.

Lamar Alexander, the Secretary of the United States Department of Education, sent Florence a letter in October 1991 congratulating her on the Saudi Reading Center project – for opening wider the window of understanding on the cultures of the world.

The new Center, which opened in Jeddah in 1994, is reported to be successfully providing unique and valued services to Saudi children, parents, teachers and other adults. In addition to testing and tutoring both children and adults to improve their reading and comprehension, for the first time in Saudi Arabia, the Center:

- Provides orientation workshops on children's special needs and assessments, for public and private school teachers;

- Provides routine vision and academic readiness screening for new students of private schools; and

- Serves as a forum for a number of institutes to provide parenting skills and other educational programs for parents.

One of the ten Saudi women who participated in the training program at the GWU Reading Center said to Florence in a recent communication: "The knowledge and skills that you provided to the group no one can take from us; it will be always the highlights of our lives. Thank you."

Florence says, "The opportunity to have worked in Saudi Arabia and helped with educational programs there has made me feel that my career has, indeed, been rewarding."

---

**UNITED STATES DEPARTMENT OF EDUCATION**

THE SECRETARY

October 15, 1991

Dr. Florence L. Hesser
Director, The Reading Center
George Washington University
School of Education and
   Human Development
2021 K Street, NW, Suite 720
Washington, DC 20052

Dear Dr. Hesser:

Congratulations on the opening of the Reading Center's Saudi Arabian educational project. In a world that is in constant change, it is imperative that nations build bridges of understanding and partnerships to the benefit of the global community.

Literacy is not just about the written word, it is not just the ability to read, speak, and understand one's own language; it is also a window of understanding on the cultures of the world. Your project is opening that window ever wider.

AMERICA 2000, President Bush's strategy for reaching the National Education Goals in the United States, will certainly benefit by your efforts to expand the reach of literacy and lifelong learning across the globe.

The cooperative effort between GW and Saudi Arabia to inspire present and future literacy professionals is a tribute to the friendship we share between our two nations.

Keep up the good work.

Sincerely,

*Lamar Alexander*

Lamar Alexander

---

## Chapter Fifteen

## Privatizing Collective Farms

Leon's crowning achievement between September 1995 and his retirement in September 2000 was a key role in transforming the State-owned collective farms in Ukraine to private ownership by the farms' workers and pensioners. What a remarkable swan-song! Who could have predicted the possibility of such an event a decade earlier?

The downfall of Communism and the breakup of the Soviet Union into the various republics in the early 1990s caught much of the world by surprise. The economic plight of the Soviet Union before the breakup was worse than had been realized by the outside world. The Soviet currency collapsed completely within a week and people's life savings became worthless, state companies ran out of money, closed their doors and millions of people lost their jobs.

But the people are tough – they had seen worse during the twentieth century – and they will make the transition to a market economy work, especially the young people.

Leon had a small taste of the changing situation in Russia in September 1991. As noted in Chapter Ten he had gone with Florence, to carry her briefcase, to a conference of educators at Sochi on the Black Sea. A few days after they arrived, word got around that Leon had a background in agriculture. He was invited to dinner by the Manager of a 25,000-acre state farm in the area. Florence went along; it was a lovely setting in a nice little restaurant overlooking the Black Sea. The Manager brought three of his deputy managers and two interpreters.

The Manager wanted to talk about how the farm economy operates in America. He asked questions like, "Who tells your farmers what crops to plant?"

Leon would say, "No one tells American farmers what crops to plant; they decide that themselves."

"Who tells your farmers when to sell their crops?"

Again, Leon said, "No one tells our farmers when to sell their crops; they decide themselves when and where to sell their produce."

"Who sets the price?"

"The *market* establishes the price – supply and demand."

For the Russian farm manager these were totally unfamiliar concepts. But he knew that dramatic changes were in store in the Russian economy and he was trying to get a basic understanding of how the American system works.

Subsequently, Leon saw the situation first-hand in Ukraine where he made 23 trips on assignment between 1995 and 2000. A brief overview history provides a perspective. Ukraine gained independence from the Soviet Union in 1991; it became a sovereign country – it was no longer *the* Ukraine as a region of some other entity.

Throughout much of its history the borders had been elastic and parts if not all of Ukraine were claimed by different countries. A typical joke among Ukrainians illustrates the point. An old man who died was met at the pearly gates by Saint Peter who said to him, "Where were you born?"

The man answered, "In Romania."

"Where did you go to school?"

The answer: "In Poland."

"Where were you living when you were married?"

"In Russia."

"Where were you living when you died?"

"In Ukraine."

Saint Peter said, "You really got around didn't you."

The old man answered, "No sir, I never left home."

Following their independence from the Soviet Union, Ukrainians took pride in their status as citizens of this new country. But they were in for a shock: the transition from a defunct Communism to a nominal private-sector economy would be difficult for many of the people, especially the older citizens.

Ukraine, which had been the breadbasket of Europe during much of the nineteenth and early twentieth centuries, was now barely capable of feeding its own citizens.

Much, perhaps most, of rural housing late in the twentieth century was still nineteenth century – outside toilets, household water carried from village pumps. Some houses had electric lights, but electrical appliances were rare.

Farm assets had deteriorated. It is being polite to say that predominant farm technology was 1940s and 1950s. The agricultural research system was not tied into the international research system. Little new technology or management information was available to farm managers.

Among the most debilitating aspects of the new farm economy after the downfall of Communism was the lack of any concept of farm management as it is practiced in free-market economies. The managers of the large state-owned farms had been told what crops to plant, how many milk cows to keep, when and where to sell their produce.

Without the needed support, the farms soon became merely subsistence operations – producing barely enough to satisfy the basic needs of the workers and pensioners on the farms. Productivity of the workers, land, and farm animals was dismal by any measure.

The social situation for many of the people, especially the elderly, was pathetic; a common sight was that of older ladies lined up on the sidewalk of a major city street, each selling a pack of cigarettes, or even one cigarette from a pack, or a knick-knack from their home, or a piece of clothing, to earn a few kopeks to buy bread.

By 1995, Ukraine's reform-minded executive leadership gave signals that they would welcome economic development assistance from the United States aimed at moving in the direction of a market-oriented economy. The USAID Mission in Kiev put together an Agricultural Land Share Project, which was approved by Ukraine's administration, aimed at privatizing the State-owned farms. RONCO Consulting Corporation was on the list of half a dozen U.S. firms that were invited to submit proposals.

Coincidentally, Leon had been to the World Bank Book Store in Washington a few days earlier and picked up a booklet on Ukraine that gave excellent background on the economy and the need for reform. World Bank consultant Zvi Lehrman was a principal author.

When USAID/Ukraine's invitation to propose came to RONCO, Leon showed the World Bank book to Steve Edelmann and said, "Here is the background we need to write a strong proposal; I will call Dr. Lehrman and see if he is willing to serve as a short-term consultant on our proposal."

Steve gave Leon the go-ahead and Zvi Lehrman agreed.

RONCO won the work order and within a few days Leon was sent to Kiev as the advance person to look for office space, identify local staff, and hold initial discussions with Felix Shklyaruk, the Ukrainian project officer in the USAID Mission who was responsible for oversight on the project.

Dr. Conrad Fritsch, RONCO's long-term Team Leader for the project, who had several years' experience in the Baltics next door to Ukraine, was to arrive in 10 days to take up his long-term assignment.

Zvi Lehrman had arranged for Dr. Anatoliy Fesina, a senior official of the Institute of Agrarian Economy, to meet Leon at the airport. Anatoliy's son, Victor, drove Leon to the Dnipro Hotel. The next morning, Victor escorted him to Anatoliy Fesina's office where Leon explained the parameters of the project.

He said, "I need an interpreter to accompany me for the next 10 days."

Anatoliy recommended Lyudmyla Rusetska, who was a professor of English and had done work for the World Bank. That was a stroke of pure luck. She served as Leon's guide and interpreter for the next 10 days. When Conrad Fritsch arrived, Leon recommended that he hire Lyudmyla as Office Manager. He did. A couple of years later the two fell in love and were subsequently married.

Conrad and Lyudmyla together made an ideal team. Conrad had the technical knowledge and organizational skills; in addition to serving as interpreter for Conrad in important meetings, Lyudmyla soon proved to be much more than an office manager. She was superb at governmental relations – she was keyed into an invaluable network of people and information.

Conrad had a tough job: the legal and regulatory framework for privatizing farms did not yet exist in Ukraine, no methodology existed for this unprecedented task, and the political environment for land reform and restructuring was becoming increasingly conservative, especially in Ukraine's Parliament.

Conrad's philosophy, which turned out to have been correct, was "Let's keep the number of Americans in the project to a bare minimum and hire the best Ukrainian staff available to help us define and tackle the issues."

Under Conrad's guidance during the first year, the project's Ukrainian attorney worked with the Cabinet of Ministers to amend the Land Code; a

How-To Manual was developed; and six large collective farms, as a pilot effort, were successfully restructured in Sumy Oblast and Mikolaev Oblast, two of Ukraine's 25 regional oblasts, or provinces.

During the next four years, the effort was rolled out to 18 of the 25 oblasts in Ukraine and systems were developed to issue land titles, or deeds, to the farms' workers and pensioners.

On a few occasions, the American Ambassador participated in ceremonies to issue land titles. Some of the older recipients of the titles could remember when their grandfathers had owned the land. On more than one occasion, when the Ambassador presented titles to the people, tears came to their eyes.

Perhaps the most poignant story was told by Vasyl Petrinyuk from Kemilnitski Oblast, who said, "Lenin promised to give land to the peasants in 1917, but it was the Americans who showed us how to do it 80 years later."

Leon's role had little to do with the task of restructuring the former state-owned farms; he was the farm management guru. He sought ways to approach the problem of almost total absence of farm management principles and information – on how to run a farm and make it profitable.

One such effort was a series of Commodity Sector Studies for which Leon served as Coordinator. The approach was to assemble teams of four to six specialists in each commodity of interest, spend four to six weeks traveling the country to visit sites and talk with managers, then write the main conclusions and recommendations in the form of Bulletins which were translated to the native language and widely distributed.

Among the subjects were the dairy, oilseed (sunflower), food grain (wheat, barley, rye), vegetable, feed grain (corn, barley), and livestock (beef and pork) industries. The intent was to give the new farm managers useful information on which they could base their management decisions.

To set the stage for detailed articles of the dairy industry bulletin, Leon wrote in the preface something like:

*As our team drove from Kiev to Sumy, I observed: 'This land is like that of Iowa; this is not dairy land.' Yet, every farm has a large herd of 'dual purpose' cows – intended to produce both beef and milk – which are tended by upwards of 30 milkmaids. By western standards, the yield of milk from each cow is* abysmally low. And there are more than 400 dairy processing plants in the country.

I predict that by the year 2020, assuming that Ukraine remains on the track toward a market-oriented economy:

- Land like Iowa's will have shifted to produce only higher-value crops and will have very few dairy cows;

- The more rolling land, suitable mainly for hay and pasture, similar to that of upper New York State or Wisconsin, will become the land of new breeds of high-producing dairy cows;

- The region of sand hills, where less palatable forage grows, will become the land of new breeds of beef cattle; and

- There will be no more than 20 or 30 dairy processing plants in the country.

The problem is, how do we get there from where we are today; but by 2020, if I am still around, I will be 95 and will be unaccountable!

One project meeting, in Sumy Oblast in 1997, was attended by two enterprising managers of farms that were among the first to be restructured; one of these managed the very first farm for which land titles had been issued. They said to Leon, "We would like to go to America and visit some farms."

Leon thought to himself, *Sure, lots of people would like to go to America.*

The two followed up with, "We will pay our own way; all we need is an invitation so we can get a visa."

Thinking that even if they had an invitation, they would not likely be issued a visa, Leon said, "No problem; I can get you an invitation." Then, he added, "If you come to the States during this 10-day window in October, I will drive you around the country to visit some farms."

Leon drafted an invitation for Steve Edelmann to sign; he signed it and sent it to Kiev.

Lo and behold, the two got up at 4 a.m. to stand in line at the American

Embassy and they got their visas. Leon met them at the airport in Washington, DC. For the next 10 days he escorted them and an interpreter to visit a dozen farms in Indiana that were owned and managed by his contemporaries when he was farming years earlier.

They also visited a couple of farms in Virginia. Leon says this was one of the most memorable occasions in his life; undoubtedly, it was also a highlight for the Ukrainians. Without exception, the American hosts opened their arms and hearts to the visitors who were served more coffee, donuts and apple pie than they otherwise would have experienced in a lifetime.

*Ukrainian farm managers Mykola Kostyuchenko (left) and Volodymyr Golynskiy enjoy coffee and dessert in a hospitable Indiana farm home, 1997*

More importantly, the Ukrainians marveled at the technology and efficiency of the farm operations. As but one example, the first farm they visited in Indiana was the same one that Leon had farmed for five years – from 1947 to 1952.

It was now owned and operated by Matt Dirkson, an energetic 30-year-old who, together with his wife and one hired man, farmed about 500 acres and milked 175 cows in a modern, computerized milking parlor. The Ukrainians shook their heads in amazement. A similar-sized operation in Ukraine would have 25 or 30 milkmaids and farm workers.

Shortly after the two Ukrainian farm managers returned to their home-land, one of them – Mykola Kostyuchenko – was asked by President Kuchma to serve on his panel of agricultural policy advisors, presumably at least partly so he could share his experiences in the United States.

Another sub-project that Leon spearheaded was a pilot effort in Lviv Oblast, which adjoins Poland in the west of Ukraine. The project hired enterprising Deneil Parker, an Iowa farmer with experience in Ukraine, as day-to-day manager of the activity.

As one activity, Parker introduced sweet corn, which had been unknown in the area. Small-scale farmers successfully grew it; some was sold as a fresh vegetable in local markets, but mostly it was processed and marketed by a local company that had been processing peas. The project helped transform the state-owned processing company to private ownership by a combination of the company's workers and farmer-growers of peas and sweet corn.

The Lviv project staff held seminars and one-on-one sessions to intro-duce farm management principles and helped start 4-H clubs, among other activities.

During one 18-month period of the Agricultural Land Share Project, Leon volunteered to serve as Head, Monitoring and Evaluation Section. Florence joined him in Kiev for much of that time. Together, they enjoyed attending some of the magnificent productions of opera, ballet and sym-phony in the beautiful and newly redecorated Opera House, and at the Philharmonia near their apartment. They enjoyed walks together along charm-ing Kraschatuk Street, Kiev's equivalent of New York's Fifth Avenue, and dining in some of the city's many fine restaurants.

Florence recalls Kiev as "the mother of Russian cities" because it was the first capital of the three main Slavic peoples: the Russians, the Ukrainians, and the Byelorussians. With its gilded domes of mediaeval churches and monasteries, Kiev is one of the most beautiful cities in the world.

But during the twentieth century, Kiev was probably affected more by historical events than any other European city: German occupation during World War I, the cataclysm of the revolution, the horror of the Stalin-in-duced famine, the terror years, and the second German occupation with its bloodbath during World War II. Then, during a period of some 40 years of relative calm, the city patched itself up and started functioning again.

After the old order crumbled, Kiev began restoring and rebuilding its cathedrals, some of which had been destroyed during the Communist era. Most others were used for secular music and theater performances. Florence especially enjoyed visiting – literally spending hours – in some of the newly restored cathedrals. Her favorite was the magnificent, 1,000-year-old St. Sophia Cathedral, with its glistening green-gold colored domes, which was within two blocks of their apartment.

She watched as replications of original life-sized murals of the disciples were painted on the walls of the foyer. She witnessed the breathtaking un-veiling of two enormous new murals outside the entrance of St. Sophia Cathedral: one depicting The Ascension and the other The Gathering of Saints in Heaven. Stalin may have closed the churches and cathedrals, but he had not squelched the people's faith.

By the end of year four, so much pressure was building in the country-side for privatizing farms and issuing land titles that the central government in Kiev said, in effect, "OK, show us how to do it."

Thus, the fifth and last year of the project was devoted largely to training a cadre in the central ministry to support and monitor teams in each oblast who, by this time, already knew how to do it.

At the peak of activities, RONCO had only six Americans but more than 300 Ukrainian employees working on the project. Except for a small but highly productive group of support staff in Kiev, the Ukrainians were out in the oblasts where the action was.

By the end of the Agricultural Land Share Project in September 2000, under those activities directly managed by project staff, 922 large farms in 18 of the 25 oblasts had been restructured into 18,000 more efficient opera-tions, some 532,000 land share certificates preliminary to land titles had been issued, and more than 239,000 land titles had been issued to the farms' workers and pensioners. Even more importantly, a system was in place so that Ukrainians themselves could complete the process of privatizing all farms in the country.

Joe Stalin would not have approved!

## Chapter Sixteen

## A Pervasive Imbalance

Since World War II, starting with the Marshall Plan to help rebuild Europe and afterward with a focus on the world's poorer countries, America has helped other nations help themselves through a variety of assistance programs. The mutually supportive purposes of these programs are to further America's foreign policy interests in expanding free markets and democracies while at the same time improving the lives of the citizens of the recipient countries. With effective programs, the United States benefits at least as much as the other countries. Countries that can feed themselves and are free and democratic make good trading partners and good allies.

U.S. foreign assistance is administered in several ways: through grants and loans directly to developing countries and indirectly through funding international organizations such as the United Nations, the World Bank and the International Monetary Fund (IMF).

America's foreign assistance that goes directly to developing countries is administered by the United States Agency for International Development (USAID), an arm of the State Department.

USAID is charged with promoting long-term development in the world's less advantaged countries. In the early 1990s, USAID began helping countries of the former Soviet bloc make the difficult transition from autocratic, command economies to democratic, free-market economies.

This book emphasizes food production, because that is Leon Hesser's perspective. Other programs – education and health, for example – also are important. Educational programs aim to reduce illiteracy. Health programs transcend a wide spectrum: vaccinating children, preventing AIDS, eradicating polio and preventing unwanted pregnancies.

The American economy benefits from foreign assistance programs in several ways. Enduring benefits are the new markets and increased trade generated for the United States. Studies show that American exports increase to those countries whose economies grow due to development assistance.

Foreign assistance helps create the stable and transparent business standards that U.S. companies must have to operate in a country. Studies also indicate that a higher percentage of U.S. export growth is from developing countries compared with traditional trading partners.

Foreign aid has never been well understood by the American general public and has tended to be unpopular. This may be one reason that, in the aftermath of the Cold War, Congress reduced U.S. foreign assistance. For a decade following 1985, the International Foreign Affairs Function of the U.S. budget was cut drastically in real terms, while domestic functions increased more than 20 percent in real terms. This sent a signal to the international community that development was no longer an American priority.

Far less than 1 percent of the U.S. budget goes to foreign aid. A poll sponsored by the University of Maryland in 2001 showed that most Americans think the United States spends about 24 percent of its budget on foreign aid.

During the Cold War foreign aid was used as a tool to contain communism. Under the Reagan administration, for example, U.S. economic and military aid reached $27 billion per year. After the Cold War it was reduced; early in the 21$^{st}$ Century it was only slightly more than one-third that level.

The United States – by far the world's largest economy – provides more foreign assistance than any other country. By that measure, Americans can be proud. But wait; as a percentage of total national income, measured by gross national product (GNP), the United States ranks *last* – 22$^{nd}$ among the world's 22 wealthiest countries. For a few select countries, following are data on official development assistance (ODA) as a percentage of GNP, compiled by the Organization for Economic Cooperation and Development (OECD).

| Country | 1999 | 2000 | 2001 | 2002 |
|---------|------|------|------|------|
| | *ODA as a percent of GNP* | | | |
| 1.Denmark | 1.01 | 1.06 | 1.01 | 0.96 |
| 2.Norway | 0.91 | 0.80 | 0.83 | 0.91 |
| 3.Netherlands | 0.79 | 0.82 | 0.82 | 0.82 |
| 4.Luxembourg | 0.66 | 0.70 | 0.80 | 0.78 |
| 5.Sweden | 0.70 | 0.81 | 0.76 | 0.74 |
| | | | | |
| 22. United States | 0.10 | 0.10 | 0.11 | 0.12 |

September 11 was a wake-up call. The global campaign against terrorism has prompted many U.S. politicians and growing numbers of the general public to entertain the view that economic and military aid to other countries, as well as a useful foreign policy tool, is a moral obligation.

A University of Maryland poll of July 2002 – after September 11 – indicated that 81 percent of Americans support increasing foreign aid to fight terrorism. That same poll indicated that Americans would like to spend $1 on foreign aid for every $3 spent on defense.

The existing ratio at the time was $1 on foreign aid compared with about $19 spent on defense. In March 2002, President Bush pledged to increase U.S. foreign assistance by 50 percent over the next three years.

The long-term commitment to development has served the United States well. A goal of American foreign assistance is to help developing countries achieve independence and self-sufficiency. The Marshall Plan that helped Europe get back on its feet quickly after World War II was a stellar example. Since then, other countries have graduated from America's assistance programs: South Korea, Taiwan, Costa Rica, Thailand.

Dramatic achievements toward reducing hunger and mitigating global poverty were made during the last half of the 20th Century, with relatively minimal investments of American resources. During the last decade of the 20th Century, USAID dramatically reduced emphasis on agriculture, on helping poorer countries become self-sufficient in food production. Among the possible reasons:

1.  Developing countries may now draw on the extensive family of international agricultural research centers for needed new technologies; this is especially true for those countries that are effectively linked

to the international centers and have national systems geared to field testing  and extending the new varieties and technologies to their farmers; however, many countries do not yet have the required national systems in place.

2. Americans may mistakenly believe that if the United States helps poorer countries produce food it will harm their ability to export farm products; on the contrary, experience demonstrates that when these countries develop, they increase their imports from America; free and democratic countries make good trading partners and good allies.

Or perhaps, as Florence says, it's because:

3. A smaller pool of agricultural experts exists in America from which to draw; the Leon Hessers – people with a solid farm background plus advanced academic training in agriculture – are a dying breed. At the beginning of the 20th Century, farmers made up 39 percent of America's population. Early in the 21st Century, it is down to 1 percent.

Whatever the reasons for decreased emphasis on helping poorer countries increase their food production, it remains that widespread hunger exists in many areas of planet Earth.  Americans need to lead the world in addressing this pervasive imbalance.

## Chapter Seventeen

## Early Morning Sights and Sounds

In November 2000, shortly after Leon had retired for the second time, at age 75, the Hessers moved to the serenity of sunny Naples, Florida. But as one might expect, Leon and Florence are only semi-retired.

During the autumn of 2001 Leon was asked to teach a course in Economics at nearby International College. The interaction with the 20 students aspiring for MBA degrees was quite stimulating – and challenging! The old man had to brush up on his college algebra and statistics, but as recompense for any shortcomings there he undoubtedly more than compensated with vignettes from his varied experiences in other lands.

Leon says, "It was a delightful experience and it gave me a better appreciation for the hard work that Florence and her colleagues had done in their college teaching careers."

In 2002 Leon was called out of retirement to make two trips to Cairo, Egypt to write some conclusions – lessons learned – for a project that he had helped start seven years earlier.

The lessons learned were written in the form of Extension Bulletins aimed at Egypt's small-scale farmers, who far outnumber the larger ones, to indicate what they can do to take advantage of the newly opened markets in Europe for their fresh fruits and vegetables.

One night each week, Florence and Leon deliver meals to shut-ins, on behalf of the Methodist Church. Florence took the required courses and qualified to be a Stephen Minister. She is frequently called on to counsel with and lend encouragement to fellow citizens in time of need.

Leon is a charter member of the local ROMEO Club: Retired Old Men Eating Out. He finished writing a book that was published in 2002: *The Taming of the Wilderness: Indiana's Transition from Indian Hunting Grounds to Hoosier Farmland: 1800 to 1875.*

Gwen, who now lives with her parents, is happily employed with the nation-wide care-giving firm, Home Instead. She takes pride in chaperoning elderly persons to doctor's appointments, or cleaning house and preparing meals for them in their own homes, or making sure they take their medications.

The Hessers are sponsoring Yuliya Kramarenko, a young lady from Kiev, Ukraine, as a three-year, live-in exchange student at nearby International College. They met Julia, as they call her, when she worked for a time as receptionist in Leon's office in Ukraine during the last half of the 1990s.

On many occasions she arranged tickets for the Hessers to wonderful productions at Kiev's beautifully restored Opera House, at the Philharmonia and other theaters and she often went with them. Recognizing that Julia was exceptionally bright and as one who had respectable English as well as fluency in both Russian and Ukrainian, but whose family situation provided limited means of support, Florence said to Leon, "Wouldn't it be nice if we could help Julia with her education?"

Everyone at International College loves her; she tutors in math and statistics and is making straight "A"s in Business Administration.

In early January 2003, the Hessers volunteered to host two Russian orphans for two weeks. They were in a group of 25 who were brought to Southwest Florida to be courted by prospective adoptive parents. In their late 70s, the Hessers had no intention of adopting, but partly because they had a built-in interpreter in Julia they would host the two older ones: Katia, a charming girl aged 9, and Slava, her 13-year-old brother.

In the group were two sets of darling twins, ages 5 and 6, who were siblings of the two the Hessers hosted. The agreement with the Russian adoption agency was that all six of the siblings were to be adopted, or none of them.

They could be with three different families as long as they were reasonably close to each other so they could visit occasionally. Two families quickly fell in love with the sets of twins. Days went by and no family had stepped forward to take the two older ones. As time grew short, Leon says he and Florence asked themselves whether they should consider adopting them.

Just three days before the group was to go back to Russia to await the processing of adoption papers, a kind family learned of the availability of Katia and Slava. They were elated. All six of the siblings were now spoken for.

In August, the three families stood before a judge in Russia as the final step in the adoption process. The judge was emotional when he heard the story. Leon and Florence volunteered to be adoptive grandparents to the six lovely children; Leon was Santa Claus for their first Christmas in America.

Even with all of these activities, the Hessers find ample time for long strolls in IslandWalk, their lovely new development in Naples, to enjoy the early morning sights and sounds of this southern paradise.

The waterfront to the rear of their home has numerous species of birds and waterfowl, some migratory, some permanent. An occasional cottontail rabbit goes hip-hopping through the neighborhood, seemingly without fear of molestation.

On rare occasions juvenile alligators sun themselves on the banks of the waterfront. An oft-repeated, delightful scene has a driver in the community stopping quietly in the middle of the street, causing other cars to wait, while a slow-moving turtle or a mother duck with a trail of ducklings crosses the street.

The Hessers regularly enjoy a variety of musical productions at the new Philharmonic Center for the Arts in Naples. The sessions cause them to reflect on the romantic times they enjoyed together while attending symphony, opera or ballet in St. Petersburg, Vienna, Moscow, Budapest, Kiev, and even Tirana, Albania.

An experience in Tirana retains a special place in Leon's memories. He told a teacher at an elementary school that he especially enjoyed music of all kinds. She invited him to witness their children playing various instruments.

Two youngsters, ages 7 and 10, played a piano and demonstrated superb technique for their ages, but the piano was terribly out-of-tune. Leon asked if there were someone in Tirana who could tune it.

The teacher said, "Oh yes, but it would cost a month's salary to get it tuned."

Leon said, "How much is that?"

"Thirty dollars; and we have three pianos."

Leon said, "Get them all three tuned and I will pay for it; just do not tell the guy that an American is paying for it."

The teachers and the principal were so pleased that they later invited Leon to a private recital in which ten students of various ages played piano, violin, and horn solos. Leon shed tears at the marvelous performances.

Sunday mornings at the North Naples United Methodist Church are a special part of the Hessers' weekly routine. The dynamic minister, Dr. Ted Sauter, has seen the congregation grow geometrically; it soon outgrew the large new sanctuary that was opened in the year 2000 so that three services are required to accommodate those attending during the season when the snow-birds have come down from the north.

The Hessers especially enjoy the music, organized and directed by Dr. Rob Newell: wonderful arrangements of choir, organ and piano music, oc-casionally accompanied by the hot trumpet of Barron Collier High School music teacher Mark Branson, or supplemented by world-renowned opera singer Steffanie Pearce.

On a recent Sunday morning while enjoying the music, Leon grinned as he had a mental flashback to Sunday mornings at the little white rural church of his boyhood and visualized Edith Yost leading the few in song with one hand on the vintage piano.

Late in the afternoon of that same Sunday, Florence and Leon watched another of the fabulous sunsets over the Gulf of Mexico as they walked arm-in-arm on the white-sand beach near the pier in Olde Naples. As the sun gave way to the fluffy, crimson clouds overhead, Leon pulled Florence closer to him and said in his succinct, matter-of-fact, straight-to-the-point style, "Sweetheart, we've come a long way since Lickskillet."